JOYCE CARY
A Reappraisal

JOYCE CARY

A Reappraisal

Dennis Hall

St. Martin's Press   New York

ISBN 0–312–44516–4

Library of Congress Cataloging in Publication Data

Hall, Dennis, 1928–
    Joyce Cary: a reappraisal.

    Bibliography: p. 157
    Includes index.
    1. Cary, Joyce, 1888–1957 – Criticism and interpretation.
I. Title.
PR6005.A77Z68   1983   823′.914   81–21463
ISBN 0–312–44516–4   AACR2

To my wife, Kit

Contents

Preface

This book, which has grown out of my belief that Joyce Cary is an unreliable guide to the meaning of his own work, began its life as my PhD thesis, which was accepted in the summer of 1978.

I am happy to acknowledge my indebtedness to Philip Yarker of King's College, London, who supervised me and gave me much good advice, to the Central Research Fund of the University of London, which gave me a grant in connection with my initial research, and to Brighton Polytechnic, where I teach, which supported both the thesis and the book with time and money. I should also like to thank my colleague, Joy Higginson, who read parts of my earliest drafts and made many valuable comments, and, above all, my wife, who not only supported and sustained me throughout as only a good wife can, but also gave me great assistance with the tedious business of checking typescripts and proofs. I am grateful to them all.

I have, of course, been careful to acknowledge indebtedness wherever I have been aware of it. Should there be any omissions, I offer my apologies and assurances of good intent in the hope they will be accepted.

Joyce Cary's work has stubbornly refused to die, yet his reputation has failed to grow, largely because, as I remember being told on one occasion, 'You don't know where to have him.' This book is an attempt to determine where he really stands, and I hope that it will at least provide fresh material for debate.

Hurstpierpoint   D.P.H.
West Sussex

Acknowledgements

The author and publishers wish to thank Curtis Brown Ltd, on behalf of the Joyce Cary Estate, for permission to quote the extracts from *To Be a Pilgrim*, *Prisoner of Grace* and *The Captive and the Free*; Mrs Winnifred Davin for permission to quote from Joyce Cary's unpublished works; and the Bodleian Library for permission to examine the James Osborne Collection of Joyce Cary's papers.

List of Abbreviations

Joyce Cary's novels, in order of publication:

AS	*Aissa Saved* (1932)
AV	*An American Visitor* (1933)
AW	*The African Witch* (1936)
MJ	*Mister Johnson* (1939)
CD	*Charley Is My Darling* (1940)
HC	*A House of Children* (1941)
HS	*Herself Surprised* (1941)
TBP	*To Be a Pilgrim* (1942)
HM	*The Horse's Mouth* (1944)
TM	*The Moonlight* (1946)
FJ	*A Fearful Joy* (1949)
PG	*Prisoner of Grace* (1952)
EL	*Except the Lord* (1953)
NHM	*Not Honour More* (1955)
CF	*The Captive and the Free* (1959)

Page references are always to the Carfax editions, save for *Except the Lord*, when the references are to the Standard edition of 1953, there being no Carfax edition of the work.

1 Introduction

This book is based upon the belief that the biggest obstacle to the understanding of the novels of Joyce Cary is Joyce Cary. He regarded himself as a man with a message. He believed that he was conveying it in his books. He was distressed that nobody seemed able to realise what it was and, towards the end of his life, sought to explain, at first in various articles and interviews and finally in *Art and Reality*. Presumably he died satisfied that he had made his point at last. Certainly, one hopes so.

To me, however, his explanations are not always helpful, and in certain respects obscure the issue rather than clarify it. As I see it, there were two Joyce Carys. One of them was the thinker who, puzzled as we all are by the phenomenon of human existence and needing a faith to live by, succeeded after several years of intense effort in producing a creed that, so far as he was concerned, accounted for that phenomenon satisfactorily. The other was the artist who produced the novels and who, in certain important respects, had different ideas. He knew, for example, that there is no satisfactory explanation. Cary himself was not aware of this. It never occurred to him that his novels might not – did not, if I am right – fully match his consciously held ideas and that his explanation of their meaning might therefore be misleading. He knew what he meant to do, and he was convinced that he was doing it.

Having said this, I want to emphasise that I do not believe that Cary the novelist was entirely at variance with Cary the thinker, or that the latter's ideas should be disregarded altogether. On the contrary, a knowledge of the essential points of Cary's thinking is a valuable and sometimes necessary tool for the interpretation of his works. It is a fault of his method that he sometimes succeeded so well in his avowed intention of keeping the subjective viewpoint from which he was writing out of his books that there is no means of knowing what it is without reference to his thinking. The point is that Cary was not an impressive metaphysical thinker and he did not always realise the implications of his thought. He needed

1

certainty in an area – the nature and meaning of human existence – in which certainty is impossible, and succeeded in persuading himself that he had achieved it. In a broadcast talk given in 1956, he said:

> I would start a book with a plan in my head; but before I had finished it, I would begin to question its significance. I could either feel it was trivial; or that it was dodging some final issue; that it was a fake. . . . I was dissatisfied with the meaning of my books; and that is, with every part of them, for style is part of meaning.
> . . . I finished several books before the first one that I published; but I never offered them to a publisher because, though they were complete in themselves, they all raised questions that I could not answer.[1]

In other words, he could not write convincingly about a world whose nature he could not account for to his own satisfaction. Eventually, however, as he says in the preface to the Carfax edition (1952) of his first novel, *Aissa Saved* (1932): 'I had found answers to my own problems.' This book was begun in 1928 and took three years to complete, but 'After that I wrote easily and quickly.'[2]

He was able to do so because his answers satisfied his conscious mind completely. The artist in him, however, who seems to have operated from some area of his mind below the level of conscious thought, clearly knew that there were no easy answers and constructed his own world.

In order to understand the difference, one needs to start with Cary's thinking, the essentials of which can be summarised as follows:[3] Cary was deeply religious but in an unorthodox way. He was certainly not a Christian, and is perhaps better described by the term 'deist' than any other. He believed that the existence of love, goodness and beauty in the world were proof of the existence of God, but that He must be powerless to intervene in the workings of the universe, since if He had the power to prevent evil and refrained from using it He would be evil himself, which by definition was impossible. The operation of the universe, he believed, was governed exclusively by the impersonal laws revealed by science. There are no supernatural factors. Evil therefore results only from three causes: sheer bad luck, natural disaster, and the conflict of will amongst men. There is no revelation. Man's only knowledge of God is his intuition of love, goodness and beauty. 'The actual nature of God is inconceivable to human minds.'[4] There is no after-life.

The weaknesses of this line of thought are apparent enough. The existence of love, goodness and beauty are plainly not proof of the existence of God: at best, they are no more than suggestive; at worst, they can be accounted for equally well in other ways. The assertion that He cannot intervene supernaturally denies man the possibility of achieving knowledge of His existence, since such knowledge is necessarily dependent upon revelation. This powerlessness, which leads to the assertion that God cannot be responsible for evil, also leads directly to the conclusion that He does not exist, for if He is, by definition, the creator of the universe, omniscient and omnipotent, He must also be responsible for everything that happens in it and able to intervene at will. It is possible to conceive of a God who, for reasons known only to Himself, refuses to intervene, but not of one who is powerless to do so. All the implications of Cary's thinking lead inexorably to the conclusion that God does not exist, yet his faith was unshakeable.

The second, and central, major facet of Cary's thinking is his belief that man is free and, as a necessary result, creative. He distinguished freedom from liberty, which he regarded as mere absence of restraint, and defined it thus: 'Real freedom is a man's power to do what he likes; that is to say, to form his own purpose.'[5] He recognised, of course, that in practice this power is always subject to constraint and that absolute freedom is a mere notion, but he held that 'so long as he is conscious and able to form a purpose or direct the least of his actions'[6] a man always has some freedom, because, and in this he followed Kant, man's will is itself a first cause. He saw freedom as both a blessing that was responsible for all man's joy and a curse that caused all his sorrows. To him, the perpetual struggle to enlarge his power to do what he likes is man's fundamental activity. His world, he said in an interview broadcast in 1955, was that of 'the free personal soul making up his mind about things, if you like, creating his own world by his imagination'.[7] From this activity arises that conflict of wills which is one of the sources of evil. Thus the price of freedom is everlasting turmoil.

As with his religious convictions, Cary was unshakeably convinced that he was right, and so he may be, but there is no proof.

One may, and arguably must, act upon the assumption that one is free, but the determinists may still be right for all that their argument is so unpalatable.

The third major aspect of Cary's thinking is his conception of morality and, as in the case of religion, his thinking on the subject turns out to be contradictory. To begin with, he shared the belief that 'all moral problems are unique. . . . The moral world consists entirely of exceptions.'[8] He did not believe that life is, or can be, lived completely in accordance with codes of conduct. His article 'Political and Personal Morality'[9] makes this plain. It is necessary on occasion both to tell lies and to break promises, and if the end is good the action is justified. He believed also that because man is free he is necessarily moral and he ascribes the steady progress that he saw in history, 'from the rigid and often cruel enforcements of arbitrary dictates, to the consideration of the individual case', to 'the moral sense of mankind, the intuition of goodness, of right, of true justice', for 'It is that which is prior to all relations, to all codes of law, which transforms them all and survives them all.' The possession of freedom allied to the intuition of love, beauty and goodness, must mean that man by nature seeks the good, and that therefore 'all choices are moral choices' and 'Moral action is always purposeful. . . . It seeks to avoid an evil consequence and ensure a good one.'[10]

The implications of Cary's thinking are interesting. It follows, for example, that there can be no such thing as an intrinsically evil man. This is consistent with his view that other than from natural causes and bad luck, evil arises only from the conflict of will amongst men, which in turn arises from the self-evident fact that individual intuitions of goodness, right and true justice will vary, one man's good being another man's evil.

However, if man by nature always seeks to do good, then it follows that he is not a moral being within the normal meaning of that term, since the concept of moral conduct must comprise the possibility of choosing to do evil. Take away the power to choose this course and morality disappears: man becomes amoral. The idea of what is good then ceases to depend on intuition of a God-based ideal form and becomes instead merely that which gives satisfaction, just as evil becomes that which causes dissatisfaction, to the individual.

What Cary calls moral action is thus, ultimately, only action intended to give personal satisfaction. Disinterested action of a self-sacrificial nature becomes impossible, since a person apparently performing such an action necessarily incurs the pain involved only in the expectation of some greater good. Freedom, in Cary's sense, also becomes impossible. If man's characteristic activity is a search for satisfaction, since he is not author of himself he cannot be free to do what he likes. I shall amplify this point a little later.

There can be no doubt that, once again, Cary did not realise the implications of his thinking. His unshakeable belief in God and in Platonic intuition could not but prevent him from realising that he had destroyed conventional morality, conceived in terms of transcendental standards.

The reason for my earlier dismissal of Cary as a thinker and also for Professor Molly Mahood's observation, made in a broadcast talk in 1977, to the effect that Cary's vision is in some ways an amoral one,[11] will now be apparent. It will also be apparent that Cary really did have a curiously divided mind. He believed devoutly in a personal God, but logically he ought to have been an atheist. He was convinced of the existence of transcendental values, but he ought to have been an existentialist. He was convinced that man is free, but for practical purposes he was a determinist. He was similarly convinced that man is moral, but his world is essentially an amoral one. He was a man who could not consciously face the consequences of his own thinking, and who found it necessary to disregard its plain implications (by no means a rare achievement, of course) in order to make life intelligible, explicable and, therefore, manageable. He knew perfectly well that life as we experience it is a chaos, and said so, but at the same time insisted that it made sense.

However, the part of him that wrote the novels, the artist, did accept the implications of the thinker's ideas and worked accordingly and it is this that makes Cary the theorist such an uncertain guide to the novels. How, then, are they to be interpreted?

There can be no doubt, I think, that Cary's primary concern is with freedom. He wrote: 'All my books deal with the world which, as I see it, is the consequence of this situation [the "fact" that man is free]. I once had a plan to call the books the Comedy of Freedom . . .';[12] and on another occasion: 'My world is that of the free soul in a society in which the permanent qualities of affection are realised in a situation of continuous change. . . . All my books deal with different facets of this dilemma.'[13] His conscious purpose as an artist was thus centred on the problems that the individual encounters in trying to 'create his own world', to make his life what he personally wants it to be; and he set out in his books to explore and depict the situation that results from the efforts of different kinds of people, with different needs, in different social contexts, to achieve this kind of satisfaction. In fact, the sole concern of all Cary's fictional major characters (excluding, that is, those in *A House of Children*, who are based upon real people) is the pursuit of self-satisfaction, when self-satisfaction is defined as the product of doing what you like. There are always wider issues involved, of course: art in the first trilogy and politics in the second, to take the two most obvious examples; and these issues are treated seriously, but they never constitute the major centre of interest.

Passionately as Cary believed in freedom, he cannot be doing what he thought: depicting human beings who, in spite of constraint, are undeniably free; since it is not possible, without recourse to fantasy, to portray convincingly in fiction a state of affairs that cannot be shown to exist in reality. Moreover, a reading of his novels that is coloured neither by knowledge of his intentions, nor by the influence of any of the criticism that is based upon his statements, does not, in my opinion, leave the impression that his people are free. The opposite is the case. Cary's characters are never seen deciding what the larger purposes of their lives are to be, as one would expect if their minds are indeed to be regarded as first causes. What motivates them is always given and can always be accounted for by inherited factors and a plausible response to the environment. They never change courses or become in any substantial way different people as a result of their experiences. Rather, they go on pursuing the same ends until their deaths, which are often premature and usually a direct consequence of their conduct. In effect, Cary determines in advance what sorts of people his characters are and never lets them develop. The only freedom he allows them is that of selecting whichever seems best of the available means of attaining their ends, which is hardly an adequate demonstration of the 'fact' that man's will is a first cause.

In a writer who wants his characters to be seen as free, this is astonishing. The power of self-determination, if only on occasion, and the ability to change as a result of it are the minimum effects such a writer must create if he is to have any chance of success. It is not astonishing, of course, that Cary should have failed, since, as I say, success in his self-appointed task was in any case impossible. The astonishment arises from the complete oppositeness of the effect he produces. In *A Fearful Joy*, for example, he deliberately portrays the child of the third generation, Nancy, repeating her grandmother Tabitha's behaviour pattern, and in *The Horse's Mouth*, Gulley Jimson, as I shall show later, is clearly portrayed as a compulsive painter. It is plain enough that the thinker and the artist are not in step. There is nothing unusual, of course, about a writer who does not fully understand the nature of his own work and gives inadequate or misleading explanations of it. But as D. H. Lawrence pointed out, it is the tale, not the teller, that must be trusted.

That Cary should have been obliged to explain was, as I have said, a direct consequence of his method. He wanted his books to strike his readers as felt experience and intended that they should draw for themselves from his portrayal of life the same conclusions about what he called 'the nature of things' as he himself had drawn from life itself. That the task was beyond him, apart from the fact that he was asking a great deal, is mainly a consequence of the further fact that no book can provide the same range of information and experience that life provides. Again, he knew this and said so, but he did not take adequate steps to supply what was missing. He asked too much of his method, and did not appreciate the extent to which what was so obvious to him needed to be spelt out to his readers. In *Aissa Saved*, for example, God speaks directly to Aissa, but there is no indication in the book as to how the reader is intended to take it. Once it is known, however, that Cary denied God the power to intervene in the workings of the physical universe, it at once becomes clear that Aissa's experience must be seen as purely subjective. It is on occasions like this that a knowledge of his thinking is essential.

It will not, then, be surprising if in order to establish what Cary's novels really are about, as distinct from what they are not, I suggest that it is necessary once more to turn to his thinking, and in particular to what I shall refer to as the *Adam* interview: 'The Novelist at Work: a Conversation between Joyce Cary and Lord David Cecil', which appeared in *Adam International Review*, vol. xviii (Nov.–Dec. 1950) pp. 15–25. In this passage, which occurs on p. 18, the dual nature of Cary's thinking becomes clear.

CARY: — as I say, life is fundamentally a character of personal feelings. Feelings come first. People live by their feelings.

CECIL: And they live in order to try and get the right feelings, you mean? Or feelings of that kind, anyway?

CARY: Well, no. They've got a lot of feelings that they had to satisfy, they tried to satisfy, d'you see? . . . Now the free individual person has a character of feeling. (We can't go into how he develops it – he has – something is born in him – and of course –

CECIL: Something special to him, you mean?

CARY: Something special to him, his –

CECIL: Yes, I see.

CARY: His own set up, his own mixture, his own – his own complex of personal feelings. Of course, all these personal feelings arise in the first place out of universal Nature. He's a bit of universal Nature. But as an individual, each man uses his mind and his imagination to create a world satisfactory to himself.

The implications of this are plain. Men are born with a given set of predispositions and they spend their lives trying to satisfy them. Freedom consists of choosing the best means to this end. There is no suggestion that man determines his own ends or amends his mixture of feelings in any way. Cecil's suggestion to the effect that man is a moral being, seeking to bring himself into harmony with transcendental values, contained in his first quoted remark, is actually rejected. The grounds on which Cary regards man as free do not appear. The tenor of his remarks contradicts, rather than supports his notion of freedom.

There really can be no doubt that in Cary's world man is an amoral being whose ends are pre-determined, whose freedom is so circumscribed as to be scarcely worth the name, and whose sole motivation is self-satisfaction. But because he could not consciously accept this, any more than he could subconsciously reject it, what Cary did in his novels was to search for a means of alleviating this intolerable situation, for a means, that is, of salvation. Lionel Trilling, in his essay 'On the Teaching of Modern Literature', expressed the opinion that 'the questions asked by our (i.e. modern) literature are not about our culture but about ourselves. It asks us if we are content with ourselves, if we are saved or damned – more than anything our literature is concerned with salvation.'[14] Cary is a case in point. As an artist, he both asks and answers the question: 'Given that our lot is what it is, what must we do to be saved?' And in fact his first book, *Aissa Saved*, apprentice work though it is, is concerned with exactly that. It was published at the end of twelve years of continuous effort and in it, as he said himself, he succeeded for the first time both in clarifying his ideas and satisfying himself that they were valid and would translate into the novel form.

In embryo, everything he had to say is present in this book, and he spent the remainder of his life exploring the implications of his answer. One is reminded of Einstein, who announced his famous theory at the beginning of his career and then spent the remainder of his life exploring its implications. However, Cary's solution was not original; nor, of course, is this surprising. In science, there are no doubt innumerable discoveries still to be made, but in philosophy the fundamental problems are all insoluble, and it is likely that all possible solutions have been canvassed several times over. Certainly, Cary was no original thinker, and the answer he arrived at, in fact, is that true freedom, or perhaps the illusion of it, can only be found in complete, voluntary subjection to the will of God. It is this discovery that Aissa makes, and it is this that causes her to die in happy acceptance of her dreadful fate.

Cary, however, did not appreciate what his achievement was and, since, as he says in the preface to the Carfax edition, he edited out the thinking on which the book was based, it is hardly surprising that nobody else did either. Much was said about colonialism and missions; Cary himself, in the same preface, talks about the impact of ideas on cultures not prepared to receive them; and all these things the book is about, but they are not central. What happens to Aissa is; for she achieves freedom, complete and utter freedom, in the only way that is open to man. That is why the book is called *Aissa Saved*.

Having succeeded in stating his message (Cary held that all serious artists have one), he then settled down to explore its implications. The road to freedom that Aissa took is open to few. She is potentially a saint and has the illusion of direct access to God. But what of the rest of us? Cary saw two big obstacles that somehow have to be coped with. The first is youth, together with its concomitants, ignorance and inexperience. Aissa herself suffers badly in this respect. The second is what he called 'the fixed in nature', by which he meant primarily those human characteristics that are inherent and involuntary, the 'complex of personal feelings' he mentions in the *Adam* interview, and secondarily the fact that 'the world is this kind of world and not that'. In other words, in spite of his conviction that man is free, he recognised that determinism exists and is a factor that cannot be ignored.

The first stage of his development is therefore an examination of the problems that youth experiences. It stems directly from *Aissa Saved* and includes *An American Visitor*, *The African Witch*, *Mister Johnson*, *Charley Is My Darling* and *A House of Children*. All these books deal with aspects of this problem. All the protagonists, except Bewsher in *An American Visitor*, are very young adults, adolescents or children. Bewsher, it is true, is in his forties, but his behaviour is persistently boyish and he is decidedly immature. His physical and mental ages do not coincide. All these protagonists come to grief as the result of the single-minded pursuit of their own ends (of trying, that is, to do what they like), carried on with a profound lack of appreciation of the fact that other people as individuals, and society as a corporate phenomenon, also have their own given characteristics and are also engaged in the pursuit of their own ends, which must be both allowed for and, when necessary, deferred to. They do not understand what true freedom is; they lack the understanding necessary to cope with life as they encounter it, and disaster strikes them down before they have a chance to acquire it.

The final book in this group, *A House of Children*, is different in that it constitutes Cary's response to the problem: the necessity of education. It is autobiographical and it depicts the loving upbringing of the young that Cary himself experienced and that brought him successfully to adulthood. He was much concerned with the care of the young.

In the next stage, which contains the First Trilogy, *The Moonlight* and *A Fearful Joy*, Cary turns his attention to the problems confronting men and women who survive their immaturity and have to come to terms with their own natures, that part of themselves that, free or not, they cannot override without nullifying their own identities. In fact, the change of emphasis is not unheralded. Having rounded off his discussion of the problems of immaturity, Cary harked back to *Mister Johnson*, who, as a character, fits equally as well into the second stage as into the first; for like all the protagonists in the novels that constitute the second

group, Johnson is a type-character rather than a credible representation of a real human being. Cary described him in the *Adam*
interview as 'the artist in life', just as he described Sara as 'the nest
builder', Wilcher as 'the conservative', and Gulley as 'the Artist'.
Similarly, he conceived the four women in *The Moonlight* as types
of womanhood and Tabitha in *A Fearful Joy* as making an unvarying response to life, as I shall show when I come to discuss them in
Chapter 4.

There can be no doubt that the creation of type-characters was
not what Cary intended. In the much-quoted letter to Mark
Schorrer in reply to what he considered to be a faulty interpretation of *A Fearful Joy*, Cary proclaimed his hatred of allegory and
said, 'my characters are real people in a real world or they are
nothing',[15] but he was wrong. These protagonists are fixed quantities, quasi-allegorical characters designed to enable Cary to
explore the problems encountered by the human qualities they
personify, such as the artistic temperament in the case of Gulley
Jimson, and they have to remain fixed since, if they changed,
Cary's purpose would be frustrated. There is no choice, it seems to
me, but to conclude that in this respect too Cary did not fully
understand the nature of his own work: his purpose and method
are simply incompatible with his assumption about the nature of
his characters.

The third stage of Cary's exploration of his view of life is to be
found in the Second Trilogy. It is interesting to note in passing
that as he worked towards the final, full re-statement of the
solution to the problem that is embodied in the novel that alone
constitutes the final stage, *The Captive and the Free*, so Cary worked
through the lives of his protagonists. Starting with childhood,
adolescence and young adulthood in stage one, he covered the
whole lives of most of the protagonists in stage two, whilst in stage
three, all three protagonists are near to, and know themselves to
be near to, the ends of their lives. This is significant, I think, in
that Cary's primary concern at this point is no longer with the
constraints on freedom that have to be coped with, but with the
need for justification that men and women feel as their lives begin
to close in, the approval of their fellows for what they have
achieved, the assurance that they have behaved worthily – a need
that increases as death approaches.

It is as if the artist in Cary, having achieved Gulley Jimson, was
acknowledging that doing what you like, and surely Gulley comes

as near to that as anybody can, is not enough. Man does not and cannot exist in isolation. Gulley works only because he is a personification and not a 'real' human being, as Lord David Cecil realised. For all his immense vitality and his metaphysics too, he is not plausible because of his total self-sufficiency. Transfer him to *Peer Gynt* and he at once becomes a troll. But the stage three protagonists are once again people, and they have the human being's need for sympathy and approval. At this point, then, Cary the theorist's notion of freedom breaks down and is seen to be inadequate. In practice it is not merely external constraint that prevents man from doing what he likes but human nature. The way is now open for the artist to replace it with the definition that is implicit in *Aissa Saved*: freedom is not doing what you like, but doing what God likes.

The third stage thus follows organically from the second, as that did from the first. The callow youth gives way to the adult who seeks to express what is in him. The type-character adult who has done what he liked to the extent of his powers and circumstances gives way the credible adult character who desperately needs approval. The development is natural and convincing. So too is the characterisation. One remembers Gilbert Phelps's observation that Chester Nimmo's career 'is related with such calm conviction that it is often difficult to remember that it is not an actual biographical study'.[16] And once again, just as the second stage novels did not develop straight off the end of the first stage books, Cary going back to *Mister Johnson* and picking up for development an aspect that he had touched upon in passing, so now Cary goes back to *To Be a Pilgrim* and takes Wilcher as his point of departure, for he alone of the second stage protagonists feels the need to justify himself. Though conceived as a type and functioning as one, he nevertheless has this human characteristic. One cannot imagine Gulley asking for approval, nor, although their cases are less blatant, any of the others.

The stage three characters all fail in their quest, and one does not have to seek far for the reason. Man is a fickle and often irrational creature. His opinions are various and his judgements are inconstant, and in any case facts are often extremely difficult and sometimes quite impossible to establish to universal satisfaction. To look for justification to one's fellow men with the expectation of more than limited success is unrealistic. Full and permanent justification can only be based upon standards that are not merely fixed and unalterable, but infallible; and for such one must look to God. Thus, with the unfinished *The Captive and the Free*, we find ourselves back with Aissa. Syson, who is her counterpart, like her achieves a vision of God that sets him free, because for him too, doing what God wants and doing what he likes become one and the same thing. There is one great advance though. Aissa could only achieve freedom at the cost of life. Syson is not required to pay such a heavy price. He lives to explore the possession of freedom, though Cary, sadly, did not. One wonders what more he would have had to say.

2   The Saving of Aissa

The events in *Aissa Saved* arise from the sincere and enthusiastic but woefully mistaken efforts of a group of African converts to Christianity to spread their new religion. The missionaries who are nominally their leaders, Mr and Mrs Carr, cannot control them and in the riot that results from their attack on the pagan *ju-ju* a great deal of blood is shed and many lives lost. Aissa, whose major concern is to reunite herself and her baby with the man she regards as her husband, is the touchstone for what happens. Her age is not given, but she is always described as a girl and is clearly very immature. When her husband, a 'worthless fellow called Gajere', is imprisoned, she demands he be ransomed; and because her baby, Abba, is sickly she demands medicine she cannot pay for. She insults those who will not satisfy her demands, is beaten and put in the stocks and eventually, weak from fever and starvation, is found and taken to the Carr's mission by two of the converts.

Thus, one of Cary's subordinate themes, that of the constraint of ignorance and immaturity, is established straight away, Aissa being depicted as an extreme case in point. We are told that 'everybody was surprised or indignant at Aissa's stupidity and violence' and that 'she was the sort of girl who could not take advice and could not control herself like a sensible creature' (*AS*, p. 46). She knows what she wants from life, and her demands are, from her own point of view, perfectly reasonable, but she has no conception of how unreasonable they seem to others and no idea of how to satisfy them. Her power to do what she likes is thus exceedingly limited. But ignorance and immaturity are not the only constraints to which she is subject. What Cary described as 'the fixed in nature' also comes into play because Aissa, like all Cary's major female characters, is a nest builder, that is, a woman whose nature it is to be a wife, mother and home maker. The outstanding example is Sara in *Herself Surprised*, who spends her whole life enticing, or trying to entice, men into domesticity, but there are no exceptions. Cary saw all women as being compelled by nature to fulfil this role and later wrote *The Moonlight* to illustrate the point. To him it was a simple fact of life, and, as has several times been remarked, it emerges plainly enough from a reading of the novels. It is helpful, though, to have it in mind from the outset, since it does help to make the point that the weight of determinism on his characters is heavy. Aissa is not doing what she likes in seeking Gajere: she is doing what she must. We are not shown her forming a purpose of her own, and since all her actions are directed towards the purpose that nature has formed for her it is hard to envisage her as being in any significant way free.

But there is more to Aissa than this. She has in her 'some of the qualities of the saint', defined as 'the power to continue in the same mood of devotion for some time and to return to it at will' (*AS*, p. 152). In effect, she has access to God, to whom she can turn with perfect sincerity and the certainty of a response at any time. At first, however, her relationship with God is purely commercial: 'Every day after her conversion she had gone to the chapel, made Jesus a curtsey, and said, "I tank you Jesus, you good to me I good to you" ' (*AS*, p. 48). She is genuinely grateful and willing to return favour for favour, but no more, and when she supports the expedition to Kolu she goes more to look for Gajere than to please God. At this point she sees God as no more than a useful ally in her efforts to satisfy the demands of her nature. However, her second attempt is no more successful than the first. Once again she is separated from Gajere and ends up a starving fugitive, and once again she ends up at the mission totally defeated, this time minus a foot and having lost her baby into the bargain. Her plight is even worse than it had been when her earlier attempts to secure Gajere's release and medicine for Abba had come to nothing.

Her initial reaction, naturally enough, is to blame God, but at this point, the nadir of her fortunes, her ability to enter into a state of devotion begins to be of use to her. Though initially obdurate, she knows that in religious terms she has been at fault: 'She had done many wicked things. She had offended Jesus and God and the Holy Spirit. . . . She had brought down the wrath of all three upon Gajere and Abba. . . . She was abominably wicked . . .' (*AS*, p. 136). Her desire to punish herself by dying is evidence of repentance and duly leads to a return to grace. It is important, however, to notice how this happens. Mrs Carr's appeals are in vain; Aissa's brain is without life. The bad spirit that possesses her is washed away like sand by the music of the hymn until at last she joins in and consciously calls on Jesus. At what proves to be, in spite of backslidings, the turning point of her fortunes, Aissa is portrayed as acting in a totally involuntary manner, the music triggering a response somewhere below the conscious level of the mind. Once again, the extent to which determinism controls Cary's characters is evident.

As a result of this experience, Aissa, as the Carrs realise, attains a true idea of religion and, as a consequence of her first communion, has the first of her visions. In order to be sure of seeing these incidents in their true light, it is necessary to remember that her experiences must be purely subjective. In fact, of course, the visions are so extravagant, and Aissa herself so ignorant and hysterical, that the point is easily taken. In later books, however, this background knowledge becomes essential.

Carried by Nagulo and accompanied by her fellow-converts, Aissa now sets out on her third attempt to satisfy the demands of her nature. At the outset, the saint in her is dominant and the nest builder in decline, a reversal of the state of mind that governed her participation in the Kolu expedition. But the nest builder is a permanent part of her nature, which has not changed, and the remainder of the book is devoted to providing a solution to the problem that the existence of these two so disparate elements in her nature between them pose. The fundamental dilemma that arises from the uneasy co-existence of animal and spiritual elements in man's nature is thus a serious concern from the outset in Cary's work.

Aissa's continuance in a state of pure saintliness does not long continue. When the Christians are startled by Owule in his *ju-ju* dress and Aissa is dropped, her animal instinct for self-preservation asserts itself and she begins to crawl away. She still feels Jesus inside her, but her pure zeal for the holy war she has undertaken suddenly suffers an admixture of material considerations: 'visions of Mrs. Carr, angels, Abba, Gajere, huge pots of beer and bowls of corn, bright new cloths in all the newest stripes and the broad smiles of friends' (*AS*, p. 178) enter her mind. The progression is clear. From the experience of the communion, Aissa is moving back towards the situation at Kolu when she was briefly reunited with Gajere and her friends. The process, however, is not complete, for she expects no more at this point than to see Abba and Gajere again in heaven and, though frightened, goes to die for Jesus in combat with Owule. Her triumph and the recovery of Abba restore her momentarily to a state of saintliness as she promises her companions not only the rain that pagan and Christian alike are longing for but the Kingdom of Heaven itself. Yet it is not the pure state she had experienced earlier. The commercial element is still clearly present. She sees the recovery of Abba as a reward for her championship of Jesus, and the prompt reappearance of Gajere immediately brings about the complete re-establishment of the original business relationship between her and God, only now the implication is, 'I good to you, you good to me', another reversal of her original sentiments. It is God's turn to be grateful.

The nest builder now takes over once again. Her deal with God has been honourably concluded and she feels free to go with Gajere. As she explains to Ojo, 'I do all ting for Jesus, Ojo. Jesus tell me kill Owule. I killum. I give him ma foot. . . . I burn ma arm too. . . . Jesus say, "You good girl, Aissa. You love me proper." He give me Gajere, he give me Abba. I go home now. All done finish' (*AS*, p. 200). But just as the nest builder could not be finally defeated, so neither can the saint. The Holy Spirit reasserts itself and in response to its reproaches she gives up first Gajere, then Abba for the love of God. She gives all. Her own death certain, the saint appears finally to have triumphed, but her final vision dispels this impression. The answer to her dilemma, 'nest builder or saint?', and to man's, 'animal or spirit?', lies not in the choice of one or the other, for that is impossible in Cary's world, in which man is both body and spirit, neither being capable of existence without the other.[1] It lies in their reconciliation. Aissa sees herself going to heaven in the arms of Jesus to be united with God and permanently reunited with her husband and child. By submitting utterly to the will of God she satisfies both aspects of her nature and so achieves perfect freedom. By freely doing what she must, she at last gains the power to do what she likes.

So Cary arrives at a solution of the problem of freedom at the very outset of his career, but it is a solution that is in a very real way no answer at all, because, whilst youth, ignorance and the desire for family life are common enough, saints are too rare for their experience to be of general validity. That Cary the artist felt this is evidenced by the fact that he spent the remainder of his life working through the problem again, at enormous length, before finally being able to re-state his solution, in *The Captive and the Free*, in terms to which ordinary men and women can relate.

Although *Aissa Saved* is apprentice work with obvious blemishes – too much incident that tends to obscure what is happening to Aissa; too many minor characters with, to the European reader, confusing names that do not indicate the sex of the owner; too much noise excitement and frenzied activity that leave the reader reeling from their impact and make following the narrative thread an effort – it does embody all Cary's major themes and is in this respect too a microcosm of his world. The theme least stressed is that of man's attempt to justify himself in the eyes of his fellows which, though present in the conduct of the child Tanawe and the boy Ali, is largely bypassed by the direct appeal to their deities by Christian and pagan alike. Otherwise the question of an appeal to man scarcely arises.

The question of freedom apart, the theme that looms largest in the book is that of the constraint that ignorance places upon the efforts of men to do what they like. Paradoxically, in the case of Aissa, it has a facilitating effect, in that her ignorance of the impossibility of direct communication with God is her means of salvation, but to the remainder of the Christians, who lack her potential for sainthood, it is an enormous disadvantage. The pagan Kolua, who attempt to cause rain by the propitiation of Oke, are clearly similarly handicapped. Yet they 'are an intelligent, brave people. They know that every effect has a cause' and 'they were determined to find out why so many troubles, bad crops, bad prices, late rains one after another, had fallen upon them' (*AS*, p. 30). The ridiculousness of their conclusions is not surprising: they simply do not understand meteorology. The equally foolish notions of the Christian Africans, underlined by the fact that like the pagans they too perform a human sacrifice to their god, are equally unremarkable, since they arise from the same cause and are compounded by a totally inadequate conception of the European idea of God. The dangers of the impact of sophisticated ideas upon peoples who are not equipped to cope with them are clear enough today, though they seem to have been less so, judging from Cary's preface, when the book was written. However, the ignorance of the missionary, Carr, is worth comment, since though it is ostensibly different in kind from that of the Africans and not so readily identified, it nevertheless has much in common with it and produces similar results. It is not only the faith of the Africans that is under scrutiny.

Carr's ignorance manifests itself as a lack of knowledge of the nature of the universe. For example, when he is crossing the Niger to Kolu in pursuit of his headstrong converts, he 'felt his enemy as a personal force, as the Devil himself, penetrating, as manifold and plastic as life itself, but much more cunning' (*AS*, p. 25). This kind of thinking places him on the same plane as Aissa, for his Devil is nothing other than a sophisticated version of the bad spirit that she feels inside her on her return to the mission after the expedition. Carr does not know, as Cary and the informed reader do, that evil arises only from bad luck, natural causes and the conflict of human will, and that there is no Devil. Nor does he realise – the mere fact that he is a Christian ensures it – that there can be no direct appeal to God, and in this too he is on a par with Aissa, and is, in fact, responsible for her misconceptions. Thus the problems that arise in the book are not caused merely by the African's failure to comprehend European ideas about God, but by the failure of Europeans, in the persons of Carr and his wife, to comprehend the nature of God in the first place. Both religions, pagan and Christian, are at variance with the 'facts' on which Cary's world is based.

The inability of faith to solve the problems of this world is demonstrated by the failure of the Kolu expedition. Carr, acting sensibly, starts out with the intention of stopping it, but the singing of the hymn acts upon him with the force of a conversion and, emotionally uplifted and reproaching himself for his lack of faith, he changes his intention. 'All his hours of anxious planning, his nights of apprehension made unnecessary. Brains and nerves and courage enjoyed release like a resurrection. He did not care for anything or anybody' (*AS*, p. 29). But it is not a victory for faith, as the rapid failure of the venture demonstrates. It is a mere emotional orgy, an abnegation of responsibility that makes him responsible, though not morally of course, for the rioting and bloodshed that follows. It is suitably ironic that when the converts go off to Yanrin on the second and final expedition Carr, though wiser now, cannot prevent them because all the boats have been seized and the ferry is guarded. He has had his chance and fades indeterminately from the scene.

The only character in the book who is not obviously con-strained by ignorance is, in effect, Cary himself, in the character of

Bradgate, the District Officer. He stands in a kindly, wise, and avuncular relationship to the Carrs and the Africans alike. He knows what the bounds of possibility are and patiently labours at doing the best job he can with the very imperfect materials he has to work with. His attitudes and responses provide a yardstick against which to measure the shortcomings of the others, though he is touched in rather too lightly for this effect to be fully felt.

The existence in the book of the theme of the fixed in nature, exemplified by Aissa's uxorious characteristics, has already been indicated. Not mentioned so far, however, is the complementary question of education, due to play an increasingly prominent role in the discussion and resolution of the theme of ignorance. Cary indicates in the preface that initially, in connection with the boy Ali, it was in the forefront of his mind. Aissa and his even deeper interest in religion usurped its place, but his concern is still apparent. It appears first in the conduct of the child Tanawe, sent by her grandmother Marimi to fetch Bradgate when the Kolu expedition has been broken up and the Christians are in retreat. She is terrified, but resolute.

> She had learnt to be dutiful and to serve a common purpose. She knew that it was shameful to fail in one's duty, to be a coward, to be mean or selfish, and this knowledge, enforced by example and teaching and many slaps, had reached every part of her body so that her legs were now conducting themselves with great bravery while her mind was not so brave   (*AS*, p. 66)

Tanawe succeeds in her errand, and it is clear that she is destined to become a well-balanced member of society (it is in this way that the theme of justification is touched upon) as the result of the love and care that have been lavished upon her upbringing. The point is underlined by the conduct of Jacob who takes up her message and impudently induces Bradgate to tip him for a service that both know he has not rendered. In contrast to Tanawe, he is dressed like a white man and has had some formal education: he knows that the law forbids whites to strike him or move him by force. He knows enough to exploit the situation to his own advantage, but has acquired no sense of social responsibility to match Tanawe's. His education has been a failure.

The same may be said of Ali, who shares the characteristics of both. His sense of social responsibility is strong, and he earnestly desires to act responsibly, but like Jacob, he is failed by his education because it has not taught him that authority must be backed by power. Consequently, he assumes an authority that he cannot sustain and is destroyed by his own ignorant presumption. The three characters, minor though they are, taken together do indicate a serious concern with the question of education and the problems it entails, which is rounded off in the book, though it is no more than a temporary tying up of ends, in Chapter 39, when we are told that as a result of the Yanrin riot a niggardly extra sum of money is provided for education and that five pupils are to go to the government school at Berua to learn football, cricket and the multiplication tables. The effect of this kind of provision becomes apparent later in the person of Mister Johnson.

3 Immaturity and Ignorance

Having successfully committed his vision to paper, Cary set about refining and developing it, concentrating initially on the problems of ignorance and immaturity that had loomed so large in *Aissa Saved*, first exploring them and then providing a fully developed solution.

The first of this group of novels is *An American Visitor*. In it, Cary sets out, as he tells us in the preface, to examine the problems of a certain kind of ruler and his dilemma, and although Cary does not specify what kind of ruler Bewsher is, a reading of the book makes it clear that he is a despot with benevolent intentions, and that his dilemma is how to impose his will on his subjects given their natures and the context within which he has to operate. Quite apart from the clear evidence provided by his attitudes and actions, Bewsher is described by Gore, who in certain important respects is the touchstone by which conduct is to be judged in this book, as Bradgate is in *Aissa Saved*, as 'one of the queerest of the old gang who ruled Nigeria like independent despots' (*AV*, p. 41). In fact, Bewsher has distant affinities with Kurtz. Cary regarded Conrad as one of his masters, and his hero, like Conrad's before him, though in a much less fundamental way, has succumbed to the fascination of the jungle and the absence of restraint within it. He does not, because of his office, have the freedom that Kurtz has, nor does he have Kurtz's talents and passions. Kurtz embodies the genre: he is 'the thing itself'. Bewsher is a lesser example set in motion in a more prosaic setting. He will not willingly leave the jungle. He does his best to be a law unto himself and to have his own way in all things, and whilst he does not attempt to set himself up as a god, he does propose to foist on to the Birri his own version of Ogun, their god of thunder. Unlike Kurtz, however, Bewsher is a failure. The inhabitants of the jungle will have none of him and eventually kill him, and he arouses amused tolerance, not jealousy and hatred, among his own kind. 'At least six other men of White's standing had commiserated him to Gore. Members of the council looked sympathetic as soon as they heard his name. . . . His own resident . . . had a wonderful speech about him beginning, "Poor Bewsher, one of my oldest friends . . ." ' (*AV*, p. 39). It is, however, more usual to see Bewsher as a sympathetic figure, a kind of heroic life-enhancer battling valiantly and without rancour against the ignorance and conservatism of the Africans, the greed of the prospectors and the dead hand of bureaucracy, and dying a victim to his wife's foolish idealism. Certainly, he has a charisma that is unique in the book and is its dominant character, but a true judgement of him must be based primarily upon his success in his role as District Officer and not upon his personality. Bewsher's task is to make the process of change, which is embodied in the activities of the tin prospectors, as smooth as possible. In order to do this successfully, he needs to be aware of the wider issues involved and be prepared to play the part required of him. But this is not the case. He shows little awareness of the movement of events and acts only in accordance with his own quite unrealistic notions, which are made plain by his daydream during the sermon. As a result he is caught between the opposed forces of change and conservatism and destroyed. As a man Bewsher is charming, but as a District Officer he is a disaster. He is not an example of the able man who is inspired to that defiance of bureaucracy that is sometimes necessary for success, but an egocentric incompetent who ought to have been compulsorily retired.

There is ample evidence for this within the book once Bewsher is seen objectively, and for confirmation that so pejorative a view of Bewsher is valid, it is only necessary to turn to the article 'A Policy for Aid', which appeared in *Confluence*, vol. 4 (1955) no. 3, pp. 292–301. In it Cary supports British colonial policy in Nigeria: 'The essential points of emphasis in our administration were continuity and balance. We were not to destroy native rule and economic custom, but to develop them on their own roots; we were to aim at a general advance on all fronts including education' (p. 295). But this is not what Bewsher was trying to do. The idea of federalism is unknown to the Birri, who, with the one exception of Obai, cannot comprehend it – a fact that Bewsher cannot grasp. He has no real rapport with the Africans, and consistently treats them as children who must be bluffed into doing what he wants for their own good, thus arousing their antagonism by threatening their traditions. In his article, Cary goes on to point out that the tribal structure of African society was not only primitive but fragile and 'liable to break up at the smallest contact with new ideas' (p. 295). He gives several examples and also cites the case of an old chief who saw what he called progress,

> quite fairly, as a backward step into social confusion, crime, political strife. And it was no good telling him that these things must come, in any case, from forces which neither of us could control, from world movements of power and opinion; he couldn't grasp such a notion. He had no idea of such forces　(p. 294)

Since this is exactly the position of the Birri, Bewsher's ignorance now becomes apparent. He not only fails to understand the policy he is supposed to be administering, but is actually in the same position as the old chief, and equally unable to temper his attitude with the knowledge that 'these things must come'. He does not realise that the 'tin openers' represent 'world movements of power and opinion' that cannot be resisted. The very name he gives them indicates his lack of comprehension of the forces at work. Bewsher, if fact, must be seen as a latter-day Cnut who, unlike the original, takes himself seriously. He is not, it is true, trying to stop the tide from coming in, but he *is* trying to dictate how and at what speed it shall do it, and the attempt is equally futile.

His complete lack of awareness can be still further demonstrated by reference to the article. Cary says that 'every reform we brought in also caused dislocations or evil of some kind; and this was inevitable' (p. 294). There is no evidence that Bewsher realises this. His whole policy is designed to avoid dislocation and evil. He always visualises a smooth process of change and development as his plan for the translation of the thunder god, Ogun, into a saint of electricity, shows. He is always convinced, and this is another mark of his essential immaturity, that left to himself he can make things go smoothly; hence his attempts to avoid the telegrams from his Resident. Yet at the end of a whole list of examples of the unexpected problems that always arise as a result of even the smallest reform, Cary says that whilst such details may seem irrelevant in 1955, 'I give them because, in varying degrees of complexity, they could be paralleled in the record of every practical official' (p. 295). The clear implication is that Bewsher is not one.

Armed with this basic understanding, one can now return to the novel and see how it works, making further references to 'A Policy for Aid' as may be necessary. The situation in the book is such that the outright conservatism of the Birri on the one hand and the forces of change and all that they imply for evil as well as good on the other are in conflict, with Bewsher in between attempting to manipulate both without consulting or understanding either. He antagonises both, with the result that the forces of change, which are irresistible, threaten to destroy his career. This destruction he staves off by disappearing into the bush on the pretext of furthering Marie's anthropological studies, only to be destroyed in the end, ironically enough, by the forces of conservatism in the shape of Obai, who thinks that Bewsher is scheming the advantage of the prospectors.

The immediate cause of Bewsher's failure, however, is once again to be found in 'A Policy for Aid':

> Enthusiasm and despair, I think, both arise from a failure to ask what democracy really is, how it works, how it comes about. We see at once that it is not a formula, to be applied by proclamation, as so many liberals imagine. No blueprint for freedom has ever worked in practice. It is not even a constitution; it is more like a condition, a situation, which has arisen slowly from economic and social development (p. 298)

Although, as I have said, this article was published some twenty-two years after the book, these words might have been written as a commentary on Bewsher. He fails to ask what democracy is, and during the discussion with Cottee (*AV*, pp. 95–100), we see this happen. Cottee has been eulogising the French colonial system. Bewsher reflects:

> 'Our system is different. I wonder why.'
> 'We haven't got a system at all – no sort of principles. None of the people we send out have the faintest idea of what they are for,' [replied Cottee].
> 'I suppose not,' said Bewsher.
> But Gore could not allow his District Officer to pass over such a violent exaggeration as this. 'Isn't it one of the chief

principles to leave people to run their own affairs as much as possible? That's actually laid down in plenty of instructions and memoranda.'

'That's not a principle at all – that's just lack of intelligence. We don't even know what to do with our empire. We can't even guess what it's for' [Cottee replied]   (*AV*, p. 98)

Bewsher makes no attempt to support Gore and none to refute Cottee. He is entirely self-centred and wrapped up in his own schemes, the practicability of which he never stops to examine. He has a formula, and he does seek to apply it by proclamation, relying on personality to make his words accepted. Thus, at the gathering at Paré he makes a speech congratulating the Birri on doing what he has wanted:

And when they now sat silent he looked at them in surprise.

But Bewsher was an unaccountable person. It was impossible to know what he would do. Instead of noticing, like a Birri chief in the same circumstances, that his remarks were not wanted . . . he called out to his boy to bring him a drink and lifted it to them. 'This is health to the All-Birri.'

No one spoke. But the man was not at all disconcerted . . . and at once began to talk again, giving them the most impertinent advice about their own affairs, the affairs of the All-Birri   (*AV*, p. 167)

In fact, as the context makes clear, Bewsher does realise that his remarks are not wanted, and in drinking the toast and continuing to speak is acting his way out of a very difficult situation. Ironically, however, he is only doing what he would have done if his words had been well-received, and the knowledge that they were not makes no difference to his plans, which he never relinquishes even in the face of defeat. He is clearly unaware that 'No blueprint for freedom has ever worked in practice', and a large part of his personal tragedy arises from this fact. In spite of his undeniable charm, therefore, there can be no doubt that we must see Bewsher as an ignorant meddler, a self-satisfied menace who is quite unfit for his job, if we are to make complete sense of this book. Comparison with Bradgate (*Aissa Saved*), who is the reverse, reinforces this conclusion.

It will now be clear why I have suggested that Gore is the

touchstone. Lack-lustre and unattractive by comparison with Bewsher he certainly is, but flamboyancy is not a criterion of excellence in a colonial administrator. Effectiveness, however, is, and in this respect it is clearly Gore that the reader is intended to admire.

Once again, reference to 'A Policy for Aid' makes this perfectly clear. Compare this passage from p. 301 of the article with the passage from the novel that follows it:

> A high European official, only last year, confided to me, 'The trouble with us is that our administrative class has only two generations behind it. You, in Britain, have had such a class for centuries. . . . But we have barely started in the tradition and so our own administration is uncertain, confused, often irresponsible. It has not yet acquired the self-respect, the sense of honour, which make it a vocation rather than a career.'
>
> And the development of such a class of men who are content to devote their lives, often on bad pay and with very small recognition, to the public service, is but one step in the complex and difficult advance of a nation towards democracy.

> He [Cottee] knew Gore's family; his own had been like it; parsons, soldiers, doctors, civil servants, magistrates, none of them rich; their whole inheritance a few old swords, bibles, medals and stories; strong in that ungreedy pride which says to kings and dukes and millionaires, 'You have your part to play and I have mine'   (*AV*, p. 235)

Further passages from the novel could be cited, but they would surely be superfluous. Gore obviously is a member of the administrative class that both Cary and his 'high European official' regard as not only admirable, but also essential if democracy is to flourish. By comparison Bewsher is a dangerous *dilettante*, as is evidenced in the book by the disaster he brings about.

Gore's characteristics, inevitably, are not charismatic. He is sound, but unspectacular; cautious; too able to see both sides of a question to provide strong leadership; loyal; assiduous, but solitary by nature. Consequently he is little regarded; but it is he who, in the end, copes with the crisis. Gore is, in fact, a Cassandra-like figure: always right but never given any recognition. Apart from the instances already mentioned, his soundness is underlined by

his immunity from the anathema of starry-eyed anarchy, in the
shape of Marie. When the suggestion is made that she is preaching self-government for the Birri, Gore 'was disturbed. Self-
determination was a dangerous kind of intoxicant for conceited,
truculent savages like the Birri' (*AV*, p. 28), and the soundness of
his judgement is once again confirmed by 'A Policy for Aid'.
Speaking of Nigeria, Cary says, 'it could be added that in 1940 the
country still needed another forty years to be ready for self-
government' (p. 295). Knowing that Gore is always right makes
clear the extent to which Bewsher is wrong.

So far, I have endeavoured to present Bewsher as an essentially
ignorant and misguided man, the seeds of whose destruction lie
within himself. Like Aissa, like the Carrs and their converts, like
the Kolua, he does not understand 'the nature of things' and
suffers accordingly. But, as in the case of Aissa, Bewsher's ignorance is also linked with immaturity. He is, it is true, in his
middle-forties, but his behaviour – it is part of his charm – is
frequently boyish. His entry into the book, by means of a flying
leap in mid-Niger from a fifteen-inch wide boat on to a steamer
that was 'rushing towards [it] like a motor car' (*AV*, p. 35), strikes
a boyish note that is reinforced not only in the following para-
graphs but at intervals throughout the book. 'White, of Berua, a
senior resident going on leave' (*AV*, p. 19), speaking to Gore to
'give him a hint that Bewsher wanted looking after' (*AV*, p. 38) is
one example. 'You knew at first sight of Bewsher that he was a
man with a cause, and that he was prepared to tell you about it on
the first excuse' (*AV*, p. 39) is another. 'What have I been doing
now?' (*AV*, p. 40) are his first words to Gore. Certainly, Bewsher is
being ironic in portraying himself as a boy and, because his boyish
qualities are attractive, it is easy at this point to assume that his
detractors are at fault and that the irony is at their expense. It is
important to remember, however, that in the end it is Bewsher
who is wrong, they who are right, and that his belief that he alone
can order the affairs of the Birri successfully is essentially childish,
and typical of an immature mind. The real irony, therefore, is that
his portrayal of himself as a naughty boy is accurate.

But it is not necessary to rely solely upon the opinions of other
characters about Bewsher to establish his immaturity. His own
behaviour makes the point. 'My dear Gore,' he writes (on p. 61),
'Thanks for your efforts to save me from my youthful folly.' He is
being ironic again, but the force of it is once more against himself.

More damning, though, is his treatment of the Birri when they ask what the prospectors are doing with their surveying equipment.

'What are they doing then? What is the woman doing?'
'They are visitors come to admire your country, and intelligent well-mannered people like the Birri know how to welcome their guests'   (*AV*, p. 63)

This is so obviously untrue as to be insulting to the Africans' intelligence, but Bewsher is quite unaware of the harmful implication of his words and attitude. He is in fact playing a game of his own making, revelling in his ability to get away with it. The Birri know this and regard him accordingly as someone who is not to be taken seriously.

In Bewsher's case, however, when compared with Aissa's, immaturity has an extra dimension: Bewsher does not learn. Aissa does not either, but since her story occupies only a few weeks this is not surprising. Bewsher, though, is middle aged and, by comparison, well educated, and although the events of the story occupy, probably, a little less than a year, he has been in Africa some fifteen years and District Officer of 'his' Birri for seven or eight of them, during which time he has learnt no more about them than about colonial administration. After years of association with them he speaks their language less well than Marie does after a few months, and is as impervious to their distrust as to the soundness of Gore's advice.

As a novel, *An American Visitor* is a distinct advance on *Aissa Saved*. On one level it is indeed a study of an egocentric, despotic ruler and of his inevitable downfall. As Gore says: 'Bewsher was bound to get killed in the end' (*AV*, p. 237). At another, it is a commentary on colonial rule, on the need for sound policies and dedicated, professional administrators, on the folly of allowing undisciplined amateurs who do not understand their business to have a loose rein. At yet another, it is a demonstration of the inevitability of change and of the fact that the process can never be painless. The 'tin openers' must perform their function because they are part of the wider movement of history as well as individuals seeking to make fortunes; and the Birri's objections, one way or another, must inevitably be borne down. At all these levels Cary has something valid to say and says it effectively.

Above all this, however, the book is a study of the attempts of two human beings, Bewsher and Marie, to make life yield them the satisfaction that their natures demand, and of their refusal to accept anything less. What makes Bewsher in the end an admirable and attractive character is his good-natured determination to do what he wants and, until the end, his success in doing it. Though he is not free in the wide sense that Cary imagined, he does have the limited freedom to choose the best means of satisfying his given character of feeling, and his efforts to do so arouse the reader's sympathy, first because he is not aware of the nature of his freedom, and secondly because he is quite genuinely convinced that he is acting in the best interests of the Birri. The pursuit of self-satisfaction, perhaps better though more clumsily described as the satisfaction of the self, is not to be equated with selfishness and certainly not with hypocrisy. Though he is misguided, Bewsher is no villain.

Like Bewsher, Marie too has charm, but is not otherwise admirable. She enters the book as a dewy-eyed Rousseauian idealist who sees the Birri as the unspoilt inhabitants of a Garden of Eden and, although she is obliged by the weight of evidence to give up this particular illusion, her unchanging character of feeling has no difficulty in finding an alternative way of expressing itself. True to type, she ends the main action of the book as an equally dewy-eyed idealist who brings about her husband's death because she does not want him to do anything mean like defending himself with a gun when confronted by a disgruntled and frenzied African who is bent on murdering him. God, she is convinced, will protect his own. And in the interval between these incidents, for good measure, she has seriously suggested to Bewsher that he had been cured of poison by faith. She is patently absurd.

She does, however, appear to experience a moment of insight when, at the end of the book, she visits Bewsher's grave.

> I just had to have Birri safe for Monkey. But I didn't see that if Birri was safe, Monkey wouldn't be Monkey, and if the world was meant to be a safe place there wouldn't be any men like Monkey, and if no one was to die or suffer there wouldn't be any love, and if no one was to get killed there wouldn't be any life worth living   (*AV*, p. 237)

Reflection, however, indicates that she is once more merely idealising. It was not remotely within her power to make Birri safe and, if it had been, this could not have made Bewsher anything other than he was. He was not seeking to live dangerously, he was trying to get his own way, to 'get away with it', as he says himself when at the point of death. The necessary complement to love is not death and suffering, but hate. What makes life worth living (amongst other things, of course) is not getting killed, but the fact of death, whatever form it may take. Marie as usual, is being absurd, and her words must be interpreted as an effort, natural enough in the circumstances, to relieve herself of the guilt she knows she bears for her husband's death.

Cottee's judgement, therefore, as he looks down at her kneeling at her husband's grave, seems at first sight to be definitive. 'This ugly little woman a tragic queen, Monkey Bewsher a hero, it was absurd' (*AV*, p. 239). At one level it is. Bewsher was an amiable menace. Marie was dangerously naïve. Between them, they did a great deal of harm. And yet, Bewsher was also a fundamentally good man who sought only to do good, and whose downfall was caused by a fatal flaw in his given character of feeling; and the same may be said of Marie. Cary's deterministic view of man has some affinity, at least, with the Classical Greek concept of fate, even though Bewsher and Marie certainly do not fulfil all Aristotle's criteria. Cary's view of life, when God is left out of the reckoning, as in this book He is, is a tragic one, and Bewsher and Marie are representative figures. To this extent Cottee is wrong.

There is also another sense in which Bewsher can be seen as a hero. Although, given his nature and his situation, he was bound to be killed and, as is suggested by his last words 'You're not going to get away with it this time' (*AV*, p. 229), he seems to have had some inkling of the fact, he did confront his destiny with courage, humour and energy and, in so far as he was happy, with success. Gore regards him as one of the happiest men he has ever known, without envy and with his cause, his hobby and his attachments. In achieving a continuing state of happiness, he is a development of Aissa. Had she lived, her happiness must rapidly have faded; in fact, had she not been dying she could not have experienced it, since it was conditional upon giving all, including life itself. But in Bewsher, Cary has taken a step towards the prolongation of the experience. Death as its price is not avoided, but it is delayed, and on very attractive terms. Public failure though he is, Bewsher's private life is a huge success.

His total life thus embodies a paradox: that the price of success is failure. He succeeded in living a happy life because he followed single-mindedly the dictates of his own nature, seeking always to give himself the greatest possible pleasure and satisfaction. In doing so, he embarked upon and persisted in a course of action that was bound to end in failure; but if he had chosen a course that would have resulted in such political success as was possible, he would not have been the happy, satisfied man he was: he would have been Gore. Aissa represents a half-way stage in Cary's progress towards this position. She does not so much command success as cheat defeat of its bitterness; but Bewsher, though just as ignorant of political reality as Aissa is of the wider aspects of human relationships and the European concept of God, and just as immature in his attempts to bring the wills of other human beings into line with his own, is much more intelligent, much better informed and therefore much better equipped for the attempt. He cannot in the end get his way, because what he wants is impossible, but he can and does achieve a kind of success which, because he is blind to its true nature and cannot foresee the ruin of the Birri that his folly must end in, makes him happy whilst it lasts. And this, according to Cary, is as much as any man can reasonably expect. By worldly standards, Bewsher is just another failure, but by his own a complete success. The reader must decide which is the more important, if he can.

THE AFRICAN WITCH

Like *An American Visitor*, this book functions at various levels. At one, it is a continuation of Cary's exploration of the constraints of ignorance and immaturity, through the person of Louis Aladai and the process of his attempts to make life what he wants it to be. At another, it is an extension of Cary's interest in the problems of leadership. Aladai and his sister Elizabeth make one contrasting pair of leaders. Aladai and the boy Musa make another, even though they never come into contact with each other. Then there are Burwash, the Emir, Salé and Coker. All are rulers or would-be rulers of one kind or another, and since the exercise of authority, and in particular despotic authority, is an important way of moulding life to one's own requirements, it is not surprising that Cary is so much concerned with it.

At yet another level, the book is a study of conservatism – its value as a stabilising force in society on the one hand, and its power to thwart human aspiration on the other. In this respect, this book is the obverse of *An American Visitor*, in which change is portrayed as a force that cannot be resisted. It is the movement of history and it has a momentum of its own that dabblers like Bewsher attempt to interfere with at their peril. In *An African Witch*, however, Cary points out that change is not, like time, an ever-rolling stream. Sometimes it runs out of momentum, as is the case in Rimi whilst the action of the book is taking place. At such times, conservatism comes naturally into its own and the efforts of yet another well-meaning dabbler, Louis Aladia, to force the pace of change are equally futile. Cary is here following another of his masters, Tolstoy, in the belief that the moment makes the man, or, as in this case, the woman, for it is Elizabeth Aladai, the ultra-conservative *ju-ju* priestess, who triumphs. Cary is not succumbing to pessimism, however. Elizabeth has not thwarted the forces of change but taken advantage of a natural pause, and when they begin to move again she will be swept away.

Finally, the theme of education appears for the first time, and in this respect Aladai and Akande Tom make yet another pair of characters who throw light upon each other. Judy Coote must also be seen in relation to both.

This pairing of characters can be extended. Judy Coote and Dryas Honeywood, mind and body, clearly fit the pattern, and the movement from the one to the other on the part of Rackham echoes the major movement in the book, which is the defeat of an insecurely based and largely irrelevant concept of progress by an instinctive and deeply rooted desire to maintain the *status quo*. Rackham's jettisoning of the highly intelligent but physically unattractive Judy in favour of the stupid but physically exciting Dryas, though not exactly analogous, also reinforces Cary's point, the point that he makes so well in 'A Policy for Aid' and underlines in this book via Burwash: that most people, provided their physical needs are satisfied, do not want progress. In Rimi, in which a stable and on the whole satisfactory state of affairs exists, nobody wants it except Aladai the idealist and his mundane counterpart Akande Tom, who alone seek to escape the power of the *ju-ju*.

A further pairing occurs between Dryas Honeywood and Osi, who are both linked to Aladai and are related to each other through the crocodile swamp. Osi literally disappears into it and

Dryas is seen metaphorically by Rackham as likely to do so (see p. 193). He turns out to be a true judge, both girls being drawn to their deaths by Aladai's unwitting influence upon them. Yet another pairing is that between Coker and Mrs Pratt. In so far as the one is rabidly anti-white and the other anti-black they are counterparts. The texture of the book is thus very close, the major elements in the pattern being constantly reinforced by pairs of characters who need to be seen as such if the book is to achieve its full impact. The biggest pairing of all is that of the black and white communities who are shown to be at one in their resistance to change. The essential conflict in the book is not between black and white but between conservatism and change. When Elizabeth claims, '*Ju-ju* for English too – all tongues, all people', there is prophetic irony in her words.

There is still one more pairing that is worth noting since it also links *An African Witch* with its predecessor *An American Visitor*, and that is the pairing of Aladai with Bewsher, whose counterpart he is in certain unfortunate ways. He has been manipulated into his role by his uncle, Makurdi, whereas Bewsher acted under inner compulsion. He is a would-be ruler whereas Bewsher is an actual one. He is a failure on all counts whereas Bewsher, subjectively, is a success. The most important factor is that Aladai is a puppet who has been groomed by his uncle Makurdi to play a part that is beyond his powers. His natural character of feeling has been violated and he has the misfortune to find himself, like Henry VI, a potential ruler who does not possess to any significant extent the natural abilities necessary for the successful performance of that function. The education that he has been given in order to further his claims by making him more acceptable to the colonial whites has had the opposite effect. He is a mere pawn who has been pushed into play by his uncle, Makurdi, who, once the game has begun is seen to-be unable to play it. Only his sister, Elizabeth, is capable of manipulating him, and he has been disqualified by his education from accepting her guidance. It has also further handicapped him by fostering in him ideas and attitudes that are not only inappropriate to the situation that exists in Rimi, but also a positive disadvantage to a would-be ruler. His situation, in fact, is tragic.

In looking at the book to see how Cary embodies what he has to say about Aladai's situation in his fiction, one notices first how attention is deliberately drawn to his youthfulness. He is some twenty-one years of age, yet he is described as a youth on his first appearance in the book at the Rimi races and is usually referred to throughout as 'the boy' by the third-person narrator. When it is noticed that Akande Tom, at twenty years of age, is twice described as a man on his first appearance and that Ojo, a very minor character, is described as 'a powerful young man of eighteen', it becomes clear that Aladai's immaturity is being insisted upon.

Ignorance, of course, is a relative phenomenon. As well as Oxford, Aladai has been to an English public school, and he has a better acquaintance with European culture than the average European. He is also described by Judy Coote as having a quick sympathy, an instant response to shades of meaning and feeling, and a real capacity for friendship. But his limited experience of life and thought is crucial in the situation in which he is placed in the book. He finds himself, through no fault of his own, in a situation which he does not know how to cope with, and the book is a study of the destruction of youth and ignorance, which in Aladai's case equal innocence, by experience. It is also an anticipation of the second stage of Cary's development of his theme, in which the emphasis is upon the way in which man's life is governed by his given complex of feelings. Aladai is their obverse and illustrates what happens when a man does not have the strength to respond to his given nature and is thus diverted from his true course of action. Characters of this kind – they are essentially non-vital, life's natural failures – are sprinkled throughout Cary's novels. Wilcher's brother Edward and nephew John, in *To Be a Pilgrim*, are examples, as is Nina's son Tom, in *Prisoner of Grace*. They start confidently, but turn out not to be in command of their lives and end up totally defeated. The vital characters, such as Bewsher, are usually defeated by the world but are successful in themselves. The non-vital, of whom Aladai is the first major example, suffer inner defeat as well.

To suggest that the book embodies a struggle between innocence and experience, however, is not to suggest that there is any simple moral scheme at work. To equate, for example, innocence with goodness and experience with evil, and to see the actions of the characters as reflecting some cosmic or symbolic struggle would be quite wrong. What happens is simply that all the people in the book are preoccupied by their efforts to create their own worlds, to order events to suit their own needs and ideas, and that those who are best at it win. The question of moral justification or condemnation in terms of some external scheme does not arise. There are no villains. All the characters are sincerely convinced of the rectitude of their own attitudes and actions and the fact that the reader will disapprove of some of them is merely a reflection of his own moral prejudices, not acquiescence in an extrinsic set of values imposed by Cary.

That Aladai lacks the ability to become a successful ruler is established quite early in the book, in his conversation with Judy Coote at Makurdi's. He thinks that people can be governed by the threat of punishment. Three years ago he had stopped, or perhaps only thought he had, one of his sister Elizabeth's witch trials by threatening to go to the judge. 'She won't do it again' (*AW*, p. 24), he asserts confidently. In fact, she is doing it again at that very moment. He thinks, too, that he can control dangerous agitators like Coker: 'If Coker became a danger, if he brought in this other *ju-ju* of blood, I should put him out of Rimi', he says to July Coote, whereas, later, at Kifi, the opposite proves to be the case. He is impervious to her oblique and ironic objection: 'Off with his head' (*AW*, p. 25).

His ideas on education are equally unrealistic. He has an uncritical admiration of British civilisation and wants to impose it directly on Rimi, and once again is deaf to Judy's suggestions (and Cary's belief, expressed in 'A Policy for Aid') that this might do more harm than good:

> 'I can't understand it,' he burst out. 'Such a great people – a great civilization! And they see that I love it. Think of how I felt when I began to read English books and to hear what civilization could mean – it was like growing up thousands of years in a few months.'
>
> 'But, Louis, Rimi has a civilization of its own.'
>
> He made a quick gesture, only short of impatience by a little politeness. 'Rimi civilization! You know that it is a joke. Can you compare it with yours? – and that means all Europe. Think of the richness of the European peoples – the poetry, the music, the – the' – he waved his hand in the air – 'the greatness of every kind.' He turned on her again. 'Rimi civilization! Do you know what it is? – *ju-ju*.'
>
> 'Not all of it, Louis,' [replied Judy Coote].
>
> But he was not in a mood for argument   (*AW*, p. 24)

Aladai's naïvety and his imperviousness to any suggestion that he may be exaggerating are clear, as is his imperfect and one-sided conception of British civilisation, indicated by his rapid lapse into generalisation. 'They [the British administration] must see – they can't help it' (*AW*, p. 26) is his last word.

His failure to take Judy's and Cary's point about the necessity of building upon existing foundations emerges equally clearly a little later:

'It's too absurd – a million without schools – and Rimi civilization! Rimi! No, I love Rimi, and it is because I love it that I want to give it something worth calling a civilization.'

'But why not do it in Rimi's own language, Louis? You can always translate from English – and then your people can say that they understand Shakespeare better than we do.'

'But then –' He had once understood and laughed at this joke; he did not notice it now. He asked, seriously and anxiously, why she was opposed to English teaching.

'Because to take another people's language and literature directly may give them a feeling of inferiority, and it often takes a nation five hundred years to get over that feeling.'

'But, Miss Coote' – he sat down, puzzled – 'I don't quite see' (*AW*, pp. 25–6)

Aladai is really making the same mistake that Bewsher made, for, like Bewsher, he is politically inept; and just as Bewsher wanted to impose his own pet ideas upon the Birri, so he wants to impose a ready-made alien civilisation on the Rimi. Unlike Bewsher, however, he does not realise that he is isolated and has no chance of support from any quarter. The whites, except Judy and Burwash, whose attitude will be discussed later, despise him; his uncle, Makurdi, is only interested in making money; and Elizabeth 'was as eager as Makurdi to see Aladai emir, but for a different reason. She disliked Mohammedans almost as much as Christians, and Salé had already threatened the *ju-ju*' (*AW*, p. 36). Aladai is thus an innocent in a world dominated by self-interest. He is convinced, like many an idealistic young man with the milk still on his lips, that he alone is right and that his cause must therefore prevail. In his ignorance of reality, he is truly pathetic.

This ignorance-which-is-also-innocence also manifests itself in other ways. For example, Aladai rejects the Waziri's offer to negotiate with him: 'The Waziri had made overtures to the boy a week before. But Aladai had refused to see him, and he had said since in public that the palace gang ought to be hanged. That was why the Waziri had joined Salé (*AW*, p. 187). This may be admirable, but it is not Cary's idea of the way the world's business must be done. Undoubtedly, he would have considered, 'C'est magnifique, mais ce n'est pas la guerre', to be a fair comment on Aladai's attitude, in view of what he says in 'Personal and Political Morality'.[1] I am not suggesting that Aladai should have behaved unscrupulously with the Waziri, as Salé did. In any case, that is not the only alternative. But I do suggest that Aladai's response to the Waziri, and especially his gratuitous public statement, are further evidence of his political naïvety and essential ignorance of the mechanics of political power. The underlying point, that organisation and the winning of allies are necessary, is made both by Salé's *coup* and, principally, by the women's clubs that Elizabeth controls and is able to mobilise in the women's war which, but for Aladai's death, she was likely to have won.

Another serious manifestation of ignorance in Aladai is his failure to realise the difference between being an African among the English at Oxford and an African among the English at Rimi. When Judy Coote was first presented to him after hearing, but not seeing, him singing Schubert in a north Oxford drawing room:

> She liked, at first sight, the handsome black with his magnificent carriage. Even the colour of his skin was an attraction to her – like that of a statue. But she was surprised to find this black statue . . . animated by a quick and ingenuous mind. . . . Perhaps, if Louis had been white, she would not have been so much impressed by his intelligence, or amused by long serious discussions about such stock subjects as English poetry, German music, French art, English politics, and primitive religion   (*AW*, p. 20)

It is clear from this that Aladai had a rarity value, perhaps a slightly freakish attraction at first even to her, an intelligent and clear-sighted woman, and was used to being encouraged as such by his white acquaintances, quite unknown to himself. The point is emphasised by Fisk's reaction when Aladai mentions his English public school: 'Why, there had been a West Indian at his own private school – a very small, very black boy, blacker even than

Aladai – who had been the spoilt favourite of the whole place.'
This is unlikely to be coincidence, especially as 'in a moment,
although he did not know it, [his] whole attitude towards Aladai
was changed' (*AW*, p. 205).

Further evidence is provided by Aladai's attitude towards his
English souvenirs, placed in his room by Makurdi:

> He went to the corner, where, on the bookshelf, he kept his
> tobacco jar with the college arms, his straight-grained pipes,
> and his photographs of college friends. The captain of boats had
> written, 'Prince Aladai, from yours sincerely'; the senior scho-
> lar, 'Louis, with love'; his tutor had signed himself, 'Yours
> affectionately'; the president of the Shakespeare Club, 'Yours
> to a frazzle.' Lesser men were his affectionate, his very sincere,
> his ever.
>
> He filled his favourite pipe with a tobacco bought in Oxford
> High Street and looked smilingly at the captain of the boats. He
> had not been very clever, he read tripe and listened to trash; but
> he had been a good fellow, a good friend   (*AW*, pp. 112–13)

Aladai's attitude towards the English is thus heavily conditioned
by his limited experience of English people. Without realising it,
he had been treated as something of a pet, indulged even. But the
colonial English abroad were not the university English at home,
as it made clear by the contrast between Judy Coote and the other
whites. It is not, of course, surprising that Aladai does not know
this, and his bewilderment at his reception by them is consistent
with the disappointment of his innocent expectations.

The significance of this to Aladai's eventual defeat is that he
comes to believe that all the whites, whom he had looked to
fruitlessly for encouragement and support, were his enemies. He
is mistaken again in this: Burwash is not, but Aladai does not
understand the difference between an Englishman acting in a
private capacity, as all the others are, and an Englishman acting
in his official capacity, as Burwash is. Consequently, Aladai
thinks that the Resident is also his enemy, whereas Burwash's sole
concern is to be sure of supporting the right candidate, that is, the
one whose accession will cause the least trouble. Elizabeth, on the
other hand, knows this perfectly well. It is not surprising that she
several times refers to her brother as 'a fool boy', whom she can
easily manage.

Unlike her brother, Elizabeth is following her natural bent. She is thoroughly at home in her role and achieves both inner satisfaction and worldly success as a ruler. Much of the secret of her success is her total harmony with those she rules. Her power is real because both she and her followers believe in it implicitly and are well-satisfied with its workings. Above all, 'she had succeeded to her uncle on account of her special aptitude' (*AW*, p. 33), unlike her brother who has to rely on birth, and she is thwarted of her triumph only by Aladai's misguided refusal to meet Burwash at Dutchi. She is the focal point of the power of conservatism within the book, and is much too powerful an adversary for her puny brother. Ultimately, of course, what he is trying to do is right, but Cary's point is that merely being on the side of the angels is not enough. You have to be the better general too.

Another aspect of Aladai's weakness as a leader is highlighted by seeing him in relation to the boy Musa. Where the former has to rely upon birth and the fortuitous blocking of the spear thrust by his prayer book which allies him with the *ju-ju*, Musa, though only about twelve, is a natural leader. Diseased, half-crippled and stunted as he is, weakest of all in a gang of physical deficients, his power is undisputed. 'He did not live in the hearts of his people', as Aladai sought to do, 'but in their nervous systems' (*AW*, p. 79) as Elizabeth does. Like her he is self-made and his rapport with his followers is close because he instinctively understands their needs and how to satisfy them. Even though he has nothing to offer that his gang could not have provided for themselves, his self-confidence, his furious energy and his play-acting always produce a response from them. His role as foil to Aladai is underlined by his claim to be the son of the Emir, so that he is at once a comic counterpart to Aladai and a pointer to the qualities he lacks. Aladai wishes to educate the Rimi but has no idea of what is appropriate. Musa is constantly educating his followers, successfully, in ways that matter to them. Although he could make nothing himself, 'Musa's gang had the best bows, spears, toyguns, traps of any other in Rimi' (*AW*, p. 80). His success depends upon his complete identity with his followers. He can show them how to realise themselves and in that limited sense make them free. This is the secret of his power. Aladai completely lacks this rapport with the Rimi. He can only sing Schubert and quote Wordsworth and act as a kind of professional adviser when they have problems. In no sense is he in their nervous systems. He has

become an alien. After the Rackham incident, he puts his Euro-
peanism aside and becomes a Rimi man again, it is true, but only
to discover for himself that he is no leader. The natural powers
that Musa has are simply not there. He finds himself in a situation
that he cannot control, becomes disorientated, and is reduced by
sheer frustration to making futile gestures of defiance that amount
to suicide, whilst Musa goes on to fortune, if not fame.

Burwash, though he does not achieve the status of touchstone
that is achieved by his predecessors Bradgate and Gore, is
nevertheless another sympathetic portrait of an effective colonial
officer. He is gently satirised at times but, though no leader in the
despotic sense that applies to the other rulers in the book, he is
courteous, humane and effective. Creative leadership is not
required of him. He is there to hold the ring and to provide the
conditions in which the African society can develop, and this he
does. It is interesting to note that at one point he is contrasted with
Bewsher, though without comment.

The theme of education, which becomes dominant in the final
novel of Cary's first group, has already become apparent in the
preceding discussion of Aladai. Judy Coote's role, as the touchstone against which the inadequacy of his ideas may be judged,
has likewise been seen. The interplay between them is underlined
by their relationships with Akande Tom. Different from Aladai in
almost every possible way, he nevertheless shares his desire to use
education as a means of escape from the reactionary world that
the *ju-ju* dominates, and provides a comic commentary on
Aladai's efforts. Like him, he tries to be a European without
understanding what this entails. Like him, he tries to dress the
part, and the incongruity of his clothes upon him matches
Aladai's bizarre appearance when, after being assaulted by
Rackham, he wears his slit jacket with otherwise African garb.
Like Aladai's, his efforts to free himself are thwarted by his inability
to comprehend what is entailed. Judy is as willing to teach him as
she had been Aladai, but as powerless to help. Tom, the comic
figure, is defeated, punished, forgiven and re-united with the
society to which he belongs, whereas Aladai, pathetic rather than
tragic, is killed.

His downfall, like Tom's, stems from his failure to make himself
part of the superior, white, order of things that, in their eyes,
represents salvation. It is easy to see this in terms of racialism
alone, but whilst this element is certainly present, it is not, I think,

dominant. Dryas Honeywood, for example, has a compulsive aversion to all things African that is part of what Rackham sees as her lack of foundations, yet in spite of this she cannot help responding to Aladai as a man, even to the point of going into the bush alone (Rackham has to follow her) to warn him that the soldiers are coming. The hatred of black men that her inadequate girl's public school education has unwittingly instilled into her is the cause of her guilty conscience. Her racialism is thus not instinctive but arises from the ignorance and immaturity, the inadequacy of education, that Cary is so concerned with at this stage. Fisk's reaction at the landing stage incident when he remembers the small black boy, even blacker than Aladai, who was such a favourite at his own school, illuminates the point and indicates another, though minor, contrasting pair of characters.

At the same time, the way in which Fisk's black schoolfellow was made a pet of underlines what I have said about Aladai, who is accustomed to similar treatment, and it provides the clue to the understanding of his downfall. When it becomes plain to him, after his assault by Rackham, that he is not going to be accepted by the whites on his own terms, he reacts as any spoilt child who suffered an incomprehensible rebuff would be likely to, by rejecting incontinently the source of pain and seeking refuge in the irrational. It is not a question of racial stereotyping. The irrational is equally in evidence amongst the British. Both the Honeywoods, for example, are specifically linked with the crocodile swamp and what it stands for. Rackham knows that Aladai is intrinsically much superior to Dick Honeywood. Mrs Pratt's attitudes and conduct are every bit as reprehensible as Coker's. And although Aladai's conduct at the swamp is a more obviously unacceptable instance of irrational behaviour than any of theirs, it is the idiom, rather than the essence, that is different. By making Aladai's brain adhere consciously to reason, Cary is able to dramatise the conflict that goes on in every human being and that may not, in fact, be capable of a final resolution. The spectacle of the normally sane man temporarily mastered by emotive claptrap appealing to his religious and patriotic feelings is all too familiar, and momentarily confers on Aladai representative significance.

Other factors, of course, have contributed to his decline. He has been out-manoeuvred by the Waziri and Salé. He has been forced to admit to himself that he cannot control Elizabeth and her women. He believes the Resident to be his enemy. Certainly, he has always reacted emotionally to Rimi, and has never been able to comprehend the difference, clear to Judy Coote, between Rimi as an undefined, emotive idea, and as a reality consisting of a body of human beings with clearly defined characteristics and limited, identifiable needs; but there is nothing in this that is not consistent with his youthful ignorance and idealism; nor is it inconsistent with human nature that in his frustration he should release his energies in the form of emotion and do it, moreover, seeing that he once again regards himself as an African, in an African manner.

It also emphasises Cary's intention in this book to treat the formidable power of the irrational and the conservative over human affairs. It is not all bad. Elizabeth, and one notes how her Junoesque stature is continually insisted upon, is one of the old gods (this she demonstrates by rising, in effect, from the dead when she is poisoned) and her rule has aspects both benevolent and valuable. Her followers live a stable life; they are not oppressed by their god, provided they give it its due; and they have a source of power to which they can turn with positive expectation in their distress, as the witch-hunting scene demonstrates. They are perfectly content. But of course there is a price to be paid, which is that of passive acceptance of the *status quo*, easy enough whilst nothing better offers but impossible for very long when it does. Aladai and Tom both exemplify this. Unlike the mass of Elizabeth's followers, they have been offered something better by their contact with the European way of life. Neither, as it happens, is strong enough to escape permanently. The old gods triumph over both, but their victory, though complete in both cases, is clearly to be short-lived.

This is illustrated by the scene in which Sergeant Bouchi reads the hieroglyphics that Rubin has cut out of old tyres. The scene is comic: the ugly little sergeant a torchbearer of the human spirit? Captain Rubin an agent of progress? The idea is absurd – but only at the mundane level. Agents of progress and torchbearers do not have to be conscious of what they are doing. What matters is that the process is being continued. It is not altogether fanciful, I think, to see an analogy with the ending of *King Lear* in this scene, even after all due allowance has been made for the differences in stature and effect of the two works. In the play, in spite of the terrible destruction wrought by the powers of evil, goodness survives. In the book, in spite of the triumph of the old gods, the will to self-determination, in the achievement of which education is so potent a weapon, likewise survives. Cary's was certainly a comic vision, but he was in deadly earnest.

Cary's next book was *Castle Corner*, but I am going to leave it out of account on the grounds that within the context of his work as a whole it is an aberration. To begin with, it is only a fragment, the first part of what was intended to be a three- or four-volume continuous narrative that was never completed. It is also, as Cary realised, the remains of an unsuccessful attempt to exploit a wider theme in a more complex setting, a task for which he was not yet ready. It is an interesting failure, in that it shows him aware of the possibilities of a wider canvas, but its principal value is that it caused him to return to the path on which he had set out and continue along it. The preface to the Carfax edition makes this clear. In fact, he was not in a position to attempt a work on the grand scale until he had delivered himself of *The Captive and the Free*, by which time it was too late.

MISTER JOHNSON

In *The African Witch*, although he takes care to show that Aladai is not equal to his task and therefore cannot be expected to succeed, and to keep a glimmer of hope alive in the comic episode of Sergeant Bouchi, Cary nevertheless strikes a pessimistic note overall. The forces of conservatism win the battle, if not the war. But Cary was an optimist. He believed that although conflict and all it entailed was an unavoidable and therefore perpetual condition of human life, the human experience was continually becoming richer and more satisfying to each succeeding generation. It is thus important, as always, to see this book in the total context of his work, and to realise that his purpose in it is, amongst other things, to indicate that the process of enrichment is not automatic and is bound to suffer setbacks and reversals. In *Mister Johnson*, however, Cary continues the development of his theme in a more optimistic vein. In Bewsher, he had created a hero who was socially disastrous but personally successful, and in Aladai, one who was a failure in both respects. Now, in Johnson, he brings personal and social success together, for it is he, not Rudbeck, who is mainly instrumental in bringing to society the benefit of the road.

Johnson, in fact, embodies a major irony, for as well as being a social benefactor he is also, as a thief and a murderer, a menace against whom society must protect itself by decreeing his destruction. And beyond this there is the further irony that he is not, by intention, either. Cary conveys brilliantly in this book the sense that the relationship between cause and effect is by no means direct, for Johnson is motivated purely by the desire for self-satisfaction and the good and evil that he does are purely incidental.

His only object is self-delight; his only use for people and institutions is as food for his ego. He has no other values, loyalties or affections; he simply does whatever gives him the greatest satisfaction at the particular moment. He is egoism personified, and therefore an ideal vehicle for Cary to use in working out his belief that every man seeks to create his own world. If he had been older and therefore more experienced, if he had been better-educated and therefore more aware, if he had been in his own community of origin and therefore subject to its values, Johnson would not have been the unsophisticated, unrestrained force that he is. He would have been much less blatant in his efforts to achieve the satisfaction of his own nature, as the later protagonists of the third group are. But this time, it seems, Cary wanted to examine, in Lear's term, 'the thing itself', and to explore the consequences of the search for satisfaction in its most extreme manifestation.

To understand Johnson, it is important to realise the full extent of his self-centredness, of his essential isolation, which Cary insists upon again and again. For example, when Johnson has first suggested to the amused Rudbeck the building of a hundred-mile-long north road to connect Fada with the main Kano road,

[he] goes off in the highest spirits. He calls at the store especially to report the conversation to Ajali. Although he knows perfectly well that Ajali is not really his well-wisher, that he is a spiteful and dangerous man, he greatly prefers him as a confidant to the honest and friendly Benjamin. The reason is that Ajali can never hide his wonderment at Johnson's deeds and Johnson needs an admirer far more than a friend. He is one of those

people who scarcely notices whether he has friends or not; he
gives friendship but he has no time to ask whether he gets it. He
is too busy   (*MJ*, p. 60)

Similarly, when he has been severely beaten on the instructions of
Waziri after his final fall from grace over the illegal road fee and
Bamu goes home with her brother, we have this: ' "Where's your
girl, den?" Ajali cries, grinning. "Where's dat Missus Johnson?"
"Missus Johnson?" Johnson is surprised. He has forgotten about
Bamu' (*MJ*, p. 191). Bamu is not real to Johnson. She is merely
part of his dream, as witness his attempt to dress her in European
clothing. He is totally unaware of her as a person and there can
therefore be no link between them other than the fact that he has
paid her family to let her marry him. Rudbeck, too, though his
supposed friendship (it is all in Johnson's mind) means more to
Johnson than his relationship with his fellow Africans, is merely
part of his self-gratifying make-believe. He 'worships Rudbeck
and would willingly die for him. He thinks him the wisest, noblest
and most beautiful of beings' just because 'Rudbeck, new to the
service, has treated Johnson, his first clerk, with the ordinary
politeness which would be given to a butler or footman at home'
(*MJ*, p. 23). But the edifice he builds on this is pure fantasy:
Rudbeck is his friend; he will lend him the money to pay his debts;
he will give him an advance of pay. Johnson's interest in and
affection for Rudbeck are in fact non-existent. He too is merely a
means of self-gratification, someone whom Johnson seeks to
please because doing so enables him to please himself. Thus,
when Rudbeck goes off with his new prismatic compass to oversee
work on the road, the novelty of being alone in charge of the office
soon wears off on Johnson. There is too little scope in it. 'He hates
to be alone, especially when he might be with Rudbeck' (*MJ*,
p. 58), not because he wants his company for its own sake, but
because it is through Rudbeck, the source of power and action,
that Johnson can best find an outlet for his egoism and energy. He
admires Rudbeck's road: ' "Oh yes, sah, we want a good road in
Fada – a motor road way up north to all these bush people – get
plenty shea butter." Rudbeck is pleased and surprised by Johnson's interest in roads.' However, 'Johnson has no special interest
in roads, but he is as sharp as a child to see what pleased Rudbeck.
His enthusiasm throws out new ideas every second' (*MJ*, p. 59).
Rudbeck, who has no imagination and, unknown to himself,

founds his life upon ideas that he picks up from those he comes into contact with, is in fact Johnson's tool where the road is concerned, as he is again in the matter of his execution. There is no personal connection.

Just as he uses Rudbeck as an outlet for his egotistic vitality (the building of the road is its incidental by-product: any other fad of Rudbeck's would have served as well) so Johnson attempts to use everyone he comes into contact with similarly. Bamu he tries to use to give substance to his concept of himself as an important government official. Ajali he uses as his admirer, Gollup as his banker, the Waziri as yet another source of income, in spite of his original grandiose refusal to take bribes. He is devoid of principle. He is motivated only by the desire for self-satisfaction and progresses quite naturally from borrowing money that he has no thought of repaying, through the taking of bribes, theft, embezzlement of illegally levied taxes (though he does use the remainder on the road, of course) to murder.

Yet he is not, in terms of morality, a criminal. He never consciously intends evil, as is indicated by the fact that at his trial he claims, quite sincerely, to have regarded Gollup as his friend. In fact, he is amoral. He has no idea of right and wrong and no conception of the consequences to himself or others of his actions. Self-realisation is his only concern and it is this that makes him immediately so fascinating. He is that real-life impossibility, a man with no inhibitions. He is presented as doing in fact what the reader dare only do in fancy. Thus, when he returns to Benjamin and Ajali ready for his first attempt to steal Rudbeck's keys, oiled, wearing only a loincloth and carrying a knife:

> Ajali and Benjamin leap up in horror. Benjamin steps backwards as Johnson advances.
>
> 'Wha-a-at?' Ajali falters.
>
> 'Johnson you m-a-a-d,' Benjamin wails in a high childish voice. 'They will catch you – it is quite certain.' And he adds surprisingly, 'Do you like to go to prison?'
>
> Johnson suddenly perceives his grandeur. He has, at a stroke, become one apart, like a terror in the world. He feels the wonder and charm of greatness. He takes out the knife and carelessly feels its edge in the firelight. Ajali turns and flies; Benjamin retreats backwards, with a wondering gaze and suddenly disappears.

Johnson is astonished. He looks after them for a minute with open mouth and wrinkled forehead. He can hardly believe that it is he, Johnson, who can produce such extraordinary effects on other people. He gradually becomes accustomed to this surprising power. In half a minute he is used to it. He hollows his back, gives a short important laugh and says to old Sozy, 'They're frightened' (*MJ*, p. 73)

This is self-satisfaction of a very high order.

Interestingly, this incident constitutes a departure in Cary's work, since for the first time a character is seen learning by insight. He suddenly realises that he has the power to make the external world conform to his will, and thus afford him greater satisfaction. He makes the discovery by accident, and it results not in a modification of his conduct towards achieving what is possible without incurring disaster – in this sense he learns nothing – but in an intensification of his efforts to satisfy the demands of his ego. He can now use people for his own purposes. This point is underlined by his thoughts when, having carried out the theft successfully and got back to his own room, frightening the boy Jamesu into silence in the process, he gloats over his success:

He is drunk with triumph and excitement. He thinks of Jamesu's terror and says, 'Why you no kill him, you fool chile? Now he go talk.'

Then he thinks, 'Let him talk. I say he mad – I never go from my bed, I *swear* I never go. I swear by Gawd.' Johnson sees himself assuring Rudbeck that he is not a thief; he can even hear, in imagination, the sob of indignation in his voice and see the innocence in his own eyes. He laughs in glory. He almost hopes that Jamesu will denounce him (*MJ*, pp. 75–6)

It will be apparent Johnson is not here glorying in his villainy, and that to imagine that he is would be to miss Cary's point completely. He is glorying in his power to create his own world. The effects on other people and society at large of the exercise of this power are incidental. Johnson deserves no credit for the building of the road, nor his poetry, nor for his party-giving (a gift he shares with Mrs Dalloway). Similarly he cannot be morally censured (social censure is another, and not necessarily moral matter) for his crimes. He is simply being himself and is no more praiseworthy for his singing than the nightingale, nor blameworthy for his killing than the tiger. The question of morality does not arise.

Similarly, for all his vitality, poetry and inventiveness, Johnson at no time displays the characteristics of a free man. Admittedly, it is not possible to demonstrate from clear evidence within the book that Johnson's nature is fixed, simply because Cary was so careful not to let the subjective centre from which he wrote appear, but there are several rather unusual descriptive statements about him that seem to imply a certain involuntary element in his behaviour. For example, on p. 19, one finds this:

> Johnson, rushing to the office, is in a panic. But his legs, translating the panic into leaps and springs, exaggerate it on their own account. They are full of energy, and enjoy cutting capers, until Johnson, feeling their mood and exuberance, begins to enjoy himself and improve upon it.

Clearly, at one level this is metaphor, and very vivid it is. Johnson's animal energy is so abundant that it overcomes his dismay at being late for work, and a point is made about the irrepressible nature of his spirits: nothing can put him down for very long. But Cary has, surely, chosen a rather odd way of making his point. If man is free, then must not freedom be a quality of the conscious mind, and should we not expect to find the mind controlling the body rather than the other way about? Why, then, choose a metaphor whose literal interpretation suggests that the body controls the mind. It is not enough to assert that it is not intended to be taken literally. The literal meaning is there and will not go away. It registers in the reader's mind, willy-nilly. Cary did not have to use this particular form of words, and it is reasonable, I think, to interpret this as an instance of the artist contradicting the thinker.

The significance of this instance would be small if it were unique. However, it proves upon examination to be one of a whole series of instances in which stress is laid upon the unconscious nature of Johnson's activities. For example : ' "You seem to get a lot of work out of your gang, Johnson" [says Rudbeck]. "Dey good men – very good gang. Dey wanna make road." Johnson has no idea why his gang does more work than the others' (*MJ*, p. 161); and a little later: 'He does not need to think, "Rudbeck's road, the great, the glorious, the wonder of the world, is about to be finished and I have helped to finish it." He knows it in every muscle' (*MJ*, p. 161). The cumulative effect of these and the many other examples that occur throughout the book is to give the impression that Johnson is simply behaving naturally, and living for the immediate sensation in an almost animal-like, or rather what one imagines to be an animal-like, way. He makes no plans and pursues no ends. He has fantasies, usually about the white man's world which he does not understand, but essentially his progress through life is like that of a butterfly through a garden. His only function is to be himself.

The book is, of course, a tragedy: that of youth in one of its aspects, essentially innocent and turned loose upon the world before it has realised – or been made to realise – that nobody who wishes to live in society can do whatever he likes. It is a tragedy also in that Johnson is the innocent victim of his own social isolation, for whilst he has learnt to despise his own culture he has not learned to understand white civilisation, and as a result has no framework within which to operate. In the brave new world in which he finds himself, anything seems possible, and Johnson's happiness, which is considerable, arises from this. His conduct sets him on a path that leads to certain disaster, but his ignorance enables him to tread it joyfully. As with Aissa and Bewsher, ultimate worldly failure is compensated for by subjective success, and even, in Johnson's case, by material success too, short-lived though it is.

In this book too, as in *An African Witch*, Cary uses the device of pairing his characters. Rudbeck is Johnson's opposite in that he has no imagination, shows no initiative. All his ideas are acquired by accidental contact. By himself, as becomes apparent when the road is finished, he can do nothing. He illustrates yet another constraint upon man's notional power of freedom: that of the lack of a motivating idea. His lack is, in fact, so absolute that he is a surprising creation in the work of a man who claimed that all his characters were real people endowed with the innate power to do what they like. If Rudbeck has it, it is not apparent, and he has to be seen as a lay figure whose function in the novel is to provide Johnson with the executive power that he lacks, both in the matter of the road and in that of his death.

Sergeant Gollup, on the other hand, resembles Johnson, echoes his behaviour and acknowledges him as a kindred spirit. His success as a trader has actually given him the power to create his own world, to maintain it in existence in a way that Johnson, who lacks a steady source of wealth, cannot maintain his, and to rule it without hindrance. Hence his eccentricity in dress and conduct, and his frequent use of violence in the gratification of his ego. Lack of restraint has made him a petty tyrant, whose success depends upon the fact that the very small limits within which he operates content him. Unlike Johnson, he does not overtly menace the social order. Taken together, the two illustrate what can happen when the extroverted human ego is freed from discipline, in Gollup's case the army. There is both profit and loss. As Johnson with his road, so Gollup with his store, in spite of his extortionate profits, provides society with a benefit; but both are dangerous when thwarted, Johnson to the extent of being an actual destroyer, and Gollup, who never quite kills Matumbi, to the extent of being potentially such. By implication the point that restraint, in the form of education for life, is necessary is clearly being made. Johnson's youth and ignorance need no further underlining, but it is perhaps worth pointing out that Gollup is also remarkably immature in his conduct and that his views – what he says about 'the white man's burden' and the British Army, for example – betray considerable ignorance.

The point is emphasised by the fact that both, like their predecessors in the earlier books, are brought by their personal characteristics to a violent end, Johnson directly and Gollup indirectly. Theirs is not the way to live, and the fact that Cary portrays them with such comic gusto must not be taken to mean that they are being held up for admiration. It is necessary to remember always that Cary is not a teacher of morality but a revealer of reality. There are no norms of conduct and attitudes in his work that the reader is being invited to give assent to, but there is a view of reality underlying the comedy and it is to this that assent is demanded. Cary requires his readers to bring to his works their own experience of life. The question, therefore, is not 'How am I being directed to see?' but 'Is the view of life that is being conveyed, so far as it goes, a true one?' Johnson and Gollup in particular are of course, grotesques, comic monsters of self-centredness, and in this respect they are the forerunners of the type-characters who predominate in the second group of novels. They are not to be admired except in so far as, together with their predecessors, they embody man's desire to have life on his own terms and to have it abundantly. In social terms they are rogues, whose actions are often to be disapproved of but whose success in living their lives on their own terms compels a certain admiration. Our experience of life also compels recognition, no matter how grudgingly, of the fact that the desire to do what you like is a potent factor in human conduct, and that those who are best at it often seem the happiest.

Ignorance and immaturity, however, upon which, in these books, the selfishness and insensitivity necessary for this kind of success are seen to depend, are not constant states in man. Those who live tend to mature and usually, to a greater or less extent, find that their ignorance of life is diminished by knowledge arising out of experience. None of the protagonists in Cary's African novels lives long enough to undergo any worthwhile change in these respects, but Johnson, significantly the last of them, does show the first glimmerings of incipient maturity and the need for awareness of the world around. The incident occurs when he is in prison after his arrest for the murder of Gollup. His good-naturedness has caused him to give his shoes to Saleh, the first action that Johnson has performed in response to someone else's need:

> Johnson sits looking at his bare feet for a long time, with an air of surprise. Then he says to his nearest neighbour with a voice inviting gossip, 'That boy, Saleh – fancy him being here.'
> . . .
> 'A most surprising thing', Johnson says in wonder. 'That boy was a most influential person – the Waziri's best friend – he had great power, and now, poor chap, well, you saw him. It makes you think, friends.'
> . . .
> 'It makes you think that a chap has to look out for himself – yes, you've got to be careful'   (*MJ*, p. 202)

That is all; but Johnson's action and reflections, contrasted as they are with the invincible self-pity and selfishness of Saleh, reveal a new dimension to his character: an awareness of the need to take the world into account and an embryonic awareness of the needs of others. Hitherto, when he has given, it has always been as an act of direct self-glorification. His ensuing death prevents any development from taking place, and the full exploration of this line of thought does not occur until the third group of novels, but the questions that are raised by this incident do foreshadow a change of emphasis that takes place in Cary's next book, *Charley Is My Darling*.

CHARLEY IS MY DARLING

In this book Cary moves his treatment of his problem on a stage, and in two ways. First, after the abortive *Castle Corner* he success-fully makes the transition from African to British settings. Second, he begins to concentrate his attention on what can be done to alleviate the situation. Education was the means he had in mind. Where ignorance is in question it suggests itself, of course, and it had already surfaced in *The African Witch*, negatively, in so far as Cary's concern in that book was with its limitations and misuse. Formal education is not enough, and may even do more harm than good. Mister Johnson, however, with his flash of insight into the need for a wider awareness, opens the way to a wider concept of education – education for life – and it is this aspect that Cary is now concerned with.

His vehicle, the boy Charley, is a character who, for the first time in Cary's work, is not markedly self-centred, but wants to achieve satisfaction within the social framework in co-operation with others, and is not only aware of his need for guidance but also anxious to obtain it.

A complete new dimension thus appears in Cary's work. Charley is the exact opposite of Johnson, who has the pure, unknowing egoism of a child and never realises how alone he is. Charlie is painfully aware of his isolation and desperately wants to belong. His shaven head and ridiculous dress lead directly to his efforts to dominate the gang, but he is not interested in leadership for its own sake. His object is acceptability, but he is at such a disadvantage because of his ludicrous appearance that the heroic approach is his only hope of success. In this respect, he has affinities with Musa, even though he lacks his intense need to dominate:

> A small boy in a man's hat hurries past the lower wall of the cowhouse, his shoulders humped, his head swinging forward at

a dejected angle. As he turns up the yard his projecting ears catch the sun and shine like rubies.

Suddenly he catches sight of the three boys standing motionless in the shadow of the cowhouse. He starts, turns as if to run off, then draws himself up, thrusts out his chin and struts towards them. His listless movement of a dejected mongrel is changed into the uneasy exaggerated swagger of the same mongrel when he finds himself watched   (*CD*, pp. 22–3)

All through the book, in his relationships with the other boys, Charley acts only in response to external pressure of one kind or another. The first shilling that Lina gives him, for example, is a means of relieving the intolerable pressure of rejection: 'A boy with a shilling, or even sixpence, however despised and cut off from society, can always be sure of a welcome when he invites another boy to share it' (*CD*, p. 53). In spite of his ducking at the hands of Mort, Charley agrees to fight him solely at Basil's insistence:

Charley had been elected chief of the anti-Morton faction, by Basil, simply because he seemed to have reason to hate Morton   (*CD*, p. 214)

Charley . . . agreed to fight. . . . Basil at once became his enthusiastic friend. Yet Charley disliked Basil and felt no desire for revenge against Mort. His instinct, when abused, was to forget about it and fill his thoughts with more amusing stuff   (p. 215)

Having allowed himself to be set up as a leader, however, Charley is bound to act in character and respond to the demands of any follower who presents himself. This situation leads him to accept Ginger's invitation to take over as 'undisputed master of the Burlswood gangs' (*CD*, p. 223) and to Mort's insistence that he should lead them to burgle houses. Charley is 'much too surprised to speak . . . and it makes him uneasy to find that he is regarded as the natural provider of treats' (*CD*, p. 224). The contrast between his attitude and that of Johnson could not be greater.

He had found no great pleasure in the last expeditions; hurried, muddled, profitless and dangerous . . . and though he never allowed himself to think 'This can't go on for ever – sooner or later I'll be caught,' he felt it continuously. It was a drag on all his enjoyment   (*CD*, p. 244)

Charley's success as a leader is thus the price he has to pay for acceptance by his peers. But leadership is not what he wants and, in itself, it means little to him. What he wants, apart from being accepted, is insight into the adult world, knowledge of life and all its possibilities of richness and satisfaction. This shows in his anxiety to learn from Lomax how he can best make use of his artistic ability, in his willingness to learn from Lina Allchin what constitutes domestic good manners, and in his eagerness to explore with Lizzie the relationship between a loving man and woman. The help he gives Lina's mother in the construction of her rock garden underlines his willingness to play a constructive role. His tragedy is that he is thwarted at every turn. Lomax is ultimately right when he says: 'No one can teach drawing – or anything else' (*CD*, p. 154) (Hesse makes the same point in *Siddartha*) but he is wrong in assuming that this means that it is impossible to give guidance and encouragement to the young in their efforts to learn. Charley is naïve in his attempt to catch 'out of this grown-up expert talk something which he will be able to use: a clue to artistic glory, triumph and fame' (*CD*, p. 159), but he is right to seek an explanation of what he does not understand and he has every child's right to the best answer that can be given. It is his misfortune that 'Lomax does not even glance at Charley. He is not interested in children, but only in his painting' (*CD*, p. 161). Charley is similarly unfortunate with Lina Allchin. She does her best to help him, but she has nothing to offer him but good manners and trust, which are not enough. It is not her fault, or anybody's, that she does not understand his needs, but again, it is his misfortune. With his father absent and his stepmother useless, Charley is left to his own devices, and his attempt to form a loving and enduring relationship with Lizzie, pathetic in itself in children of their age, is a sharp comment upon the failure of the adult world to satisfy the legitimate needs of the young. So Charley too comes to disaster, and his story turns out to be yet another study in worldly failure. The mere realisation of the need for education is not enough. Being left to work things out for oneself is not enough in a society that is not tolerant of errors.

There must be guidance, and Cary's thoughts upon the nature of it formed the substance of his next book, *A House of Children*.

Apart from its role in the development of Cary's thinking on the problems of freedom, *Charley Is My Darling* is, as has always been recognised, a sensitive novel about adolescence and juvenile delinquency. In this respect, it needs to be read in conjunction with *A House of Children* in which Cary has interesting and valuable things to say about why children behave as they do. I shall return to this when I come to discuss that book.

Before doing so, however, I want to draw attention to the fact that we now have two pairs of failures: Bewsher and Johnson, who achieve a substantial degree of subjective success ('happiness' might be a better way of putting it) on the way to disaster, and Aladai and Charley, who are for the most part unhappy and bewildered. The deciding factor is self-centredness. The first two go their own ways virtually regardless of external factors, whilst the second are manipulated into their roles as leaders and are largely at the mercy of external factors. Without education for life, the ability to cope with society, defeat is certain; but if one is sufficiently self-absorbed, the journey to meet it can be enjoyable, because it is only by responding to the demands of one's personal complex of feelings that such limited freedom as is possible in Cary's world can be fully achieved. And if one does not know, as Bewsher and Johnson do not, that one is in fact doing what one must, then the illusion of total freedom is complete. But if the necessary will to this end is lacking, for whatever the reason – and in life total egocentricity is surely the exception – then frustration must ensue and the question becomes that of how to minimise it. This, it seems to me, is what Cary's next book is essentially about.

A HOUSE OF CHILDREN

In his prefatory essay to the Carfax edition volume of this book, Cary makes it clear that this novel is fictionalised autobiography: 'I am often asked if the book is autobiographical. The answer is that names, places and people are disguised, because many of the people are living. I have given myself an elder brother – why, I do not know. But I notice that this elder brother is also myself' (*HC*, p. 7). Evelyn Corner, the first-person narrator, and Harry therefore represent the young Cary. It is his education for life that is being examined, and for the first time Cary is making a study of success, his own, and seeking to determine what the necessary conditions for it are.

The most obvious condition is an affectionate and secure stable family background, within which the child can exercise his imagination, develop his feelings and learn values. Surrounded by aunts, uncles and cousins and visited by a father whose descents upon the family have the effect of setting standards to be admired and aimed at and who, when necessary, can restore potential chaos to order and harmony, as he does after Delia's elopement, the young Cary has this to perfection. It emerges strongly both from the prefatory essay to this book and that of *Charley Is My Darling*, as well as some of his other writings, such as 'A Child's Religion',[2] that the mature Cary was entirely happy about his upbringing and did not visualise anything better. By contrast, Aissa has no family background at all, nor does Johnson. Aladai has no parents and his sister and uncle are only concerned with exploiting him for their own ends. Charley has no mother, his stepmother shows only good-natured indifference towards him and his father appears only to appease the magistrates by thrashing him: quite the opposite of Evelyn's. The father admits to having no idea whether this will benefit his son or harm him and readily agrees that it could equally well do either. Bewsher is in one way the exception. He has a stable family background in England, but he is completely divorced from it in Nigeria, where it is of no effect and for practical purposes non-existent.

Alongside, and partly arising from this lack of family background in Cary's failures is the equally important factor of social isolation. I have drawn particular attention to it in the case of Johnson, but in fact all the protagonists in this group of novels, except Evelyn, are displaced persons and not subject to any codes of values existing independently of their own wills. Even Aladai, though he is back home, is no longer the Rimi man that, after being knocked into the river by Rackham, he claims to be. His Oxford experience has changed him, and he is neither European nor African. Consequently, all these protagonists have no choice but to turn inwards, and to seek satisfaction from life without reference to society. They cannot avoid offending it because, neither belonging to it nor understanding it, they cannot take it into account. In all their cases, one is reminded of Gide's dictum, delivered in *Les caves du Vatican*, to the effect that all that is needed to make a villain of a man is to remove him from his normal environment.

Evelyn on the other hand, is very much at home in his society, no matter whether it manifests itself as family, friends or servants. Consequently, he has a freedom to experiment that is denied the others, for actions that in them are criminal, in him are allowable or at any rate not punishable; and because he is not destroyed by his actions, but is loved and protected from the consequences that he should, in theory, suffer, he is able to learn and grow. Evelyn's upbringing thus provides an interesting contrast with that of Rousseau's Emil.

The evidence for the beneficence of Evelyn's education is to be found in the fact that in *A House of Children* occur certain echoes of the actions of the earlier characters, made harmless by the fact that they are not attended by disaster. This description of the group of children Evelyn belonged to, for example, is very reminiscent of the behaviour of the African Christians in *Aissa Saved*: '. . . the faces of children surround me, and all of them, shouting, laughing, weeping, furious or affectionate, are full of impatience' (*HC*, p. 13).[3] But whereas the children confined themselves to 'tearing out bell-wires by the roots' or 'digging for pots of gold under the footmark of a rainbow' (*HC*, p. 12) and were neither punished for their wanton destructiveness nor ridiculed because of their ignorance, the Africans destroyed both property and life in the attempt to give substance to their ignorance and superstition. The scale is very different, in terms of the consequences to both the perpetrators and to society, but the underlying situations are the same. The children were fortunate and the Africans not.

Again, Evelyn talks of himself as 'running with a new-laid egg, probably stolen, to make a feast' (*HC*, p. 13). Johnson, too, stole to make feasts. Evelyn, at the instigation of the red-faced boy he met at the Maylins' party, throws snow down a chimney on to the fire below, causing both material damage and injury (see *HC*, pp. 72–3). Charley's gang, at his instigation, seriously damage the Wandles' house. Evelyn and his friends 'stole boats and borrowed the saddler's pony for rides, or, on Dunvil Green, one of the grazing donkeys; which threw us against walls or into whins' (*HC*, p. 13) without fear of retribution. Charley and his friends steal cars, and crash one of them, and end up in court.

Bewsher has ideas for the development of Birri society that, though superficially attractive, are quite divorced from reality and help to bring about his death. Evelyn and Harry go through a similar process with their play, and are helped by its failure to a greater understanding of life. Aladai comes into contact with European literature and it proves to be a factor in disorientating him and making him ridiculous to the whites. Evelyn comes into contact with *The Tempest*, and though its immediate consequence is a highly derivative and mercifully unfinished epic, his sick aunt, to whom he insisted on reading it, 'did not turn me out of the room, listened to my bad verses for at least half-an-hour, and then kissed me, and congratulated me . . . warmly and affectionately'. Though his poem was filled with nothing but platitudes, this encouragement enabled Evelyn to feel 'their meaning with such new excitement that they seemed to me new discoveries' (*HC*, p. 236), so that when he was fired by his father's high diving he was able to transfer the experience from art to life:

> It [the diving] made me cry out with delight. What a triumph, what a combination of skill, courage, neatness and deliberate mastery. It seemed to me there was no grander deed than to dive like that.
>
> I don't mean that this is what I thought about diving, at the age of ten: but this is what I felt, for I can remember how lifeless, how flat, my writing seemed, or the very idea of poetry, beside the vision of my father, one moment floating through the sky, and the next darting through the green water far be-low (*HC*, p. 239)

His father is clearly being seen by him as Ariel here and his appreciation both of him and of human endeavours has been enriched because his naïve enthusiasm for poetry was not stifled.

This list of comparisons between the experience of Evelyn and his predecessors could be extended at some length. The scale and the social consequences are, as has been acknowledged, always different, but the basic situations are always the same. All the protagonists are children, experimenting with life, trying to create their worlds around them; but whereas Evelyn is accepted as a child who is still learning, protected from the consequences of his deeds accordingly, and thus enabled to achieve both subjective and material success, the others are not. They are assumed to know what life in society is and how to behave, and no one thinks of sheltering them from the consequences of their actions. The result is that they cannot have both happiness and worldly success, since they do not know how to achieve their ends without offending society, if indeed that is possible, nor do they know how to achieve a mutually acceptable compromise either by moderating their demands or by persuading society that what they want is reasonable. They seek to gratify their desires with such complete disregard for the social context that society is obliged to defend itself against them. They have all, with the possible exception of Charley, reached a point where they are no longer capable of learning socially acceptable behaviour in relation to their particular ends. They are thus dangerous, and must be prevented from doing harm in one way or another. In the violence of the African setting, this means death; in the softer English one, in which Charley is placed, it means Borstal.

The point about the ability to learn, or the lack of it, is in this group of novels, a crucial one. It is because the child Evelyn both can learn, and, helped by his very favourable environment, does so, that he is not a criminal. It is because Charley, at fifteen, wants to learn that he is a potentially valuable citizen. His lurid stories about gangsters and their molls give way to dreams of domestic bliss in 'Ammurca' and he is dangerous only as long as he is thwarted, like Undershaft in Shaw's *Major Barbara*.

Cary's general point is clear: education for life is all-important and it must start in childhood if it is to achieve its purpose. Beyond a certain age it is too late. In MS Cary 293 of the James Osborne Collection of Joyce Cary's papers in the Bodleian Library there is an unheaded and undated typescript beginning 'Education is teaching . . .'. In it, Cary says:

> . . . and the most important part of teaching is the personal influence that is why the most important part of education are the first four or five years actually before children go to school. They get an angle from their parents which lasts them for good or evil the rest of their lives. I remember a famous but sad master of a school saying to me in private – what hampers us here is our parents we cannot expect to do more with our boys than salvage   [*sic*]

It is interesting to note how firmly in line this is with current thinking in educational psychology, in which the first five years are considered to be all-important, and to remember that *A House of Children*, the last novel in this first group, was published in 1941.

With the completion of *A House of Children* Cary had said all that he had to say about ignorance and immaturity as barriers to freedom, and about education for life as a means of reducing them – and in the process paid a great tribute to his own family and to the way he had been nurtured by it. It is possibly because, rather touchingly in an age when an unhappy childhood seems almost to be a necessary prerequisite for success, Cary was unconsciously offering himself as an embodiment of his solution that he was inhibited from following it up in novel form. But there must also have been the further reason that he knew perfectly well that education alone, no matter how effective, could not provide a sufficient means to his end, even allowing for the fact that complete freedom is in any case unattainable. Besides, ignorance and immaturity are not the only constraints. There is also the question of the fixed in nature, and it was to the exploration of this that he next turned his attention.

4 The Permanent in Nature

It is clear from what Cary said in the *Adam* interview, from which I quoted on page 8, that Cary regarded human beings as fixed quantities in whose basic characters of feeling change does not occur. Superficial change is not ruled out, of course, and is bound to occur as the individual pursues the search for self-satisfaction and learns how better to succeed, but as man is made, so he remains. The fundamentals are fixed.

It is the consequences of this state of affairs that Cary next set out to explore. The result is a group of novels, including *Herself Surprised*, *To Be a Pilgrim* and *The Horse's Mouth* (the First Trilogy), *The Moonlight* and *A Fearful Joy*, all of which deal with the whole lives of their central characters. In this, they differ markedly from those of the first group, especially as all their main characters live to old age and all but two die of natural causes. They are not complementary to each other as those in the first group are, and do not have to be read as a group in order to be fully understood. This applies even to the trilogy, which Cary admitted did not work as he intended. Their point of community is that in all of them Cary is exploring the problems of a given aspect of human behaviour. His characters are types, intended to exemplify one response to life, and he himself described most of them as such. In 'The Way a Novel Gets Written' (*Harper's Magazine*, vol. CC, Feb. 1950), he says of Sara (*Herself Surprised*):

> Give her for material almost any man and any sort of domicile and she set about building her nest. . . . Her morals were the elementary morals of a primitive woman, of nature herself, which do not change. . . . She was a female artist who was always composing the same work in the same style, but it is a style which does not go out of fashion (p. 92)

Sara thus personifies what Cary saw as an essential feminine characteristic, and her response to life is not only invariable, it is also inevitable and involuntary. By definition she cannot, and in the book she does not, respond to life in any other way. The circumstances in which she operates change, but she herself remains constant.

Just as Sara is the nest builder, so Wilcher (*To Be a Pilgrim*) is 'the Conservative,'[1] fighting for his life against change'.[2] Cary asserts that Wilcher is doing so because he is imaginatively attached to the life and things that he knows, that he is, in fact, a 'real' human being and not a personification; but, though it is true that he is much less obviously a type-character than some of the others in the group, the difference between Wilcher and them is one of degree rather than kind in that he too makes a fixed response to life.

The case of Gulley Jimson (*The Horse's Mouth*) is quite unequivocal. He is the artist and he cannot be anything else. In his introduction to the braille version of the book Cary says: 'The horse's mouth is not Gulley, but the voice that commanded him to be an artist and keeps him at it.'[3] The nature of the voice is not discussed. The involuntary nature of Gulley's artistic activity, however, is clear. He too is conceived as a fixed type, and there is ample evidence within the book to corroborate this.

The central characters in *The Moonlight*, the three sisters and Ella's daughter Amanda, are similarly conceived. Here is Cary discussing the book, again in 'The Way a Novel Gets Written'. His purpose, he says, was

> to show the woman's special dilemma in different generations, the means by which, in different social periods, it might be solved. And I wanted also to show the relation between these devised expedients, or moralities – what is often called the convention of a time – and the fundamental quality of a woman's life, imposed upon her sex, her natural powers, and her natural place in a society which contains, like herself, both primary elements from nature and a secondary social and political form   (p. 88)

It is clear from this that Cary sees woman as a fixed quantity whose basic response to life is unvarying. Thus, these characters are not four women, but four aspects of woman, and they live by making their set responses in a changing social setting. Taken together, they add up to woman as Cary visualised her.

The final protagonist in this group is Tabitha (*A Fearful Joy*), whom Cary discussed with Lord David Cecil in the *Adam* interview.

> CARY: Well now, she resents change; and the very fact that she's got a sort of dogmatic morality and not a great deal of imagination.[4] She resents change, and she gets sort of run down on the mudbanks several times . . . and that's where the crook Bonser comes in . . . every time she gets stuck down he comes and floats her off . . . this contact with him transforms, all life is revived in her again.
>
> CECIL: So in fact, she really did like the change Joyce.
>
> CARY: When she got it she hardly knew . . . but as an old woman, looking back, she does realise that Bonser . . . has given her life   (p. 17)

Once again, it is clear that Tabitha is conceived as a fixed quantity, as is Bonser. She never learns, never changes, and always makes the same response to a repetition of the same stimulus.

Cary's approach to characterisation in this group had, as I have said, an effect that he did not appreciate, for though he maintained that his characters are 'real people in a real world', they are not. Real people are, as a rule, variously motivated. Cary's group two protagonists are simplified versions of human beings in which the complexities of actual human conduct have been shorn away in order to reveal the nature of the fundamental drives that, in Cary's view, activate man, and they belong to the tradition of allegory. It is perhaps not surprising, in view of his complete faith in his own ideas, that he never realised what he was doing, but it is very surprising to me that his assertion has been so little queried. The result has been that criticism of these books has sometimes been misdirected. It is, nevertheless, possible to see how this state of affairs may have come about. Cary was so utterly convinced of the reality of his characters that he gave each of them a very precise, realistic identity: personal characteristics, family background, socio-economic setting, and geographical and historical placing; and this has been done so successfully as to create the illusion that they are real human beings. Cary's art of character

creation in this group can best be understood by reference to
Chaucer's art in creating the Wife of Bath. Like all characters in
medieval literature she is basically a type (la Vieille), but Chaucer
seems to have felt her situation and nature in human terms and
has endowed her with such vitality and pathos that she seems real.
Nevertheless, she is not susceptible to psychoanalysis in the way
that most characters in twentieth-century novels are. Cary, at a
lower level, has done the same thing. His most successful
characters have what he would have described as 'jump', and so
much so that they seem real, even though their behaviour is
purely formulaic. The most obvious case is that of Tabitha and
Bonser. He is really little more than a device for reviving her
when, because of changed circumstances, she has lost impetus,
and is so very predictable as to become a little tedious.[5] She is
interesting, however, because the reader wants to see what the
outcome will be this time, as Cary intended. But what happens
depends, as always, upon the changed circumstances that prevail
rather than upon her ability to produce a new response. In fact,
she is really a nest builder like Sara. She tries with Bonser and
fails; succeeds first with Sturge and then Gollan; has very indifferent success with her own son and his family; succeeds with
Bonser at the second serious attempt; and finally fails with her
granddaughter Nancy and her family. She ends the book at the
point of death, but still eager for more, because her business is to
live and to fulfil her own nature. The variety of circumstances, her
varying fortunes and above all, her unquenchable spirit are what
give the book its interest. She seems fully human as one reads, and
one responds accordingly. The fact that the book covers her whole
life helps to foster the illusion and one is prevented by this very
device from speculating upon her life outside the book and realising that she could not have one. Perhaps this is one reason why the
great majority of Cary's major characters are brought either to
death itself or left at the brink of the grave, with the certainty that
their next step must take them into it. In the second group,
Amanda is the sole exception.

The world of Cary's second group is thus a very sombre one,
dominated by fixed nature and characterised by limited response,
exceedingly limited freedom and amorality. Cary would, unquestionably, have been shocked, and probably outraged, to hear it
described so. Nevertheless, it does embody his basic vision of the
plight of man. The artist in him was not deceived by the inad-

p. 9). But Sara has always known what she really is and, implicitly at least, why she behaved as she did. The incident of the mirror on p. 10, when she sees herself 'with the world's eye' for the first time establishes this. She has no illusions about what she sees but is incapable of changing. When her husband suggests that her hat is unsuitable: 'I was going to say "Yes, indeed," but instead the words popped out: "No, it's not the hat – it's the glass. . . ." ' Her reply is involuntary, and she concluded, correctly, to herself: 'If I am a body then it can't be helped, for I can't help myself.' It is true that she goes on 'So I would think in those days; whenever I wanted to please myself; even against my husband' as if to intimate that she did not really believe the excuse for herself she was making, but the next sentence gives her away: 'Yet I meant to be as good as my vows and better' (*HS*, p. 10). What she tried to persuade herself was an excuse was in fact the truth; she could not help herself, and the whole of the rest of her life proves the point, in spite of the fact that at the end of her book she says she will 'keep a more watchful eye, next time, on my flesh, now I know it better' (*HS*, p. 220). This supposed new access of self-knowledge and the resolution it gives rise to, however, are mere words, for in *To Be a Pilgrim* and *The Horse's Mouth* her conduct is in no way changed. How could it be, in view of what Cary himself says about her and in view of the lengths to which he goes in the book to establish the instinctive nature of her way of life?

Sara is clearly amoral. Laws and standards of social conduct are meaningless to her. 'Her morals were the elementary morals of primitive woman, of nature herself' (see p. 62): that is, she did not have any, any more than the foal she so aptly likened herself to. She is a criminal, but she is not a villain in terms of moral culpability. When she claims to have been shocked at the judge's strictures on her she is telling the truth, and when the judge says that she has 'behaved like a woman without any moral sense' (*HS*, p. 9) he is telling the truth too, for that is just what she is. She goes through life doing the only thing she can do: attract a man and build a nest; and if she cannot confine herself to one man at a time, and entertains Hickson and Gulley Jimson whilst still married to Matthew Monday, it is not to satisfy her greed for sex, money and social position, but because she simply cannot help exercising her gift for nest building on any likely man who comes along. Besides, the benefits to her husband of these relationships (Hickson's social and financial connections and the portrait Gulley was to paint), whilst they certainly do not justify her conduct in terms of social morality, do gratify her own instinct to make a nest for him, as well as keeping men in reserve for herself should he disappear from the scene. In this she resembles her literary ancestress, who is not Moll Flanders, as some have suggested, but the Wife of Bath, as Wright first noticed,[6] even though she lacks the Wife's breathtaking belligerence and self-awareness.

This does not mean that Sara is not 'cunning, vain, lecherous, self-deceiving' (*HS*, p. 8) as Gulley also sees her, but it does mean that she is not morally guilty of these vices since she has not acquired them consciously nor does she consciously practise them. They are merely incidental to her response to the demands of her nature, and inimical to the demands of Gulley's.

What has been said about Sara must also be said about Gulley Jimson (*The Horse's Mouth*), and indeed about all the other protagonists in this group. Gulley's father was an artist whose style went out of fashion and who, in consequence, ceased to be able to sell his work. Explaining how he became an artist himself, Gulley says: 'I never meant to be an artist. You say, who does. But I even meant not to be an artist because I'd lived with one', and he explains about his father. Therefore 'I hated art when I was young, and I was very glad to get the chance of going into an office.' He then describes himself as a happy clerk with a wife and child.

> But one day when I was sitting in our London office on Bankside, I dropped a blot on an envelope; and having nothing to do just then I pushed it about to try and make it look more like a face. And the next thing I was drawing figures in red and black, on the same envelope. And from that moment I was done for   (*HM*, pp. 60–1)

It is important that what sets Gulley off is a chance incident of the most trivial nature and not a major experience, for it is precisely the very triviality of the stimulus that indicates the innate and compulsive nature of his urge to paint. He is not an artist by choice but the servant of the horse's mouth, 'the voice that commanded him to be an artist and keeps him at it' (see p. 63). But what is this voice? Gulley is no Saul on the road to Damascus. He receives no revelation, undergoes no conversion, does not even become convinced that painting is his vocation. The impression

that Gulley is programmed by nature to be an artist is overwhelm-
ing. Remarks that he makes himself reinforce it:

> Of course, I was a bad case. I had a bad infection, galloping
> art   (*HM*, p. 61)

> I was so wretched [over his art] that I hardly noticed when we
> were sold up and my wife went off, or even when my mother
> died   (*HM*, p. 62)

> I was like a chap under witchcraft   (*HM*, p. 64)

Innate ability and predispositions to given courses of action are, of
course, a perfectly normal part of human nature. We do not make
ourselves. But the way in which Cary hammers home the fact of
Gulley's utter subservience; emphasises, albeit humorously, his
privations; makes him warn off Nosy Barbon; makes Nina sus-
pect that he would be glad to give up painting if he could, and
finally makes Gulley so completely indifferent to the fate of his
walls, even to the point of continuing to paint one that is being
demolished, goes far beyond normality.

Wilcher (*To Be a Pilgrim*) is a similar but much less extreme
case. He is conceived as a conservative and remains true to type to
the end, as he himself acknowledges in the last two short chapters
of the book, but all his life he was constantly planning to live
differently: to be a pilgrim in fact. In this he differs radically from
Gulley, to whom no other life is conceivable, and is a complete
contrast to Sara, whose imperfect awareness of her own nature
comes late and only then in the context of a newspaper confession.
Wilcher has been aware all his life of the possibility of being other
than he is and has professed to desire it – in his preparation for
Holy Orders and the missionary life, for example, in his excur-
sions into Liberal politics (though family influence is at work
here), in his admiration for his sister Lucy's unorthodox life, and
in his plans to marry Sara, his housekeeper, which, as Noble
points out,[7] would in itself have been an unorthodox action. He
has also done his best to accept change, when it is presented to
him as an accomplished fact, as in the cases of the felling of the
trees and the vandalising of the Adam drawing room by Robert,
for example. But in spite of all this, he is not a conservative by
choice, but by nature, and it is for this reason that all his plans and

attempts come to nothing. He lacks the power to carry them out. This is made apparent early in the book, when he utters a thought that strikes the keynote of all that is to follow: 'Possessions have always been my curse. I ought to have been a wanderer, too, a free soul' (*TBP*, p. 16). He is already an old, sick man, and there is pathetic irony in what he says, but by the end of the book, which by implication is also the end of his life, he has come to know himself. The whole of the last two chapters are his credo.

> I walk upon the fields of the whole island [Great Britain], as upon my own carpet, and feel the same exasperation against them, for being a perpetual burden on my regard; I love the noble buildings as I loved these old chairs and tables, with anxiety and irritation. For I know very well that they are not being properly looked after. I love this island as I loved Tolbrook; and tremble for it; and perhaps I shall he happy to get some peace from both of them. They have broken my heart between them. . . .
>
> The truth must be confessed, that I am an old fossil, and that I have deceived myself about my abilities. I thought I could be an adventurer like Lucy and Edward; a missionary. I shouted the pilgrim's cry, democracy, liberty and so forth, but I was a pilgrim only by race   (*TBP*, pp. 341–2)

– and not by nature. The words scarcely need to be added. Wilcher knew of the idea of freedom; that is, he was able to conceive another and seemingly more desirable way of life than that he was pursuing; but in spite of the fact that he is Cary's most complex character, he cannot transcend the limits of his nature.

Much of the irony in this trilogy arises from the inability of the characters to realise their plight. In the cases of Sara and Gulley, this is total. At the end of her book, Sara still believes she can reform if she tries hard enough. Gulley's conviction that he is doing what he likes is absolute. Like his creator, he considers man to have fallen into freedom. Wilcher alone achieves partial knowledge of the truth, but only when he is too close to death for it to signify.

There is also much pathos in their ignorance of their situation. Poor, pathetic creatures, and, if Cary is right in his analysis of the human lot, poor pathetic mankind. But that is not to suggest that these characters are, as individuals, necessarily to be pitied. Their very ignorance shields them. Gulley is perfectly happy. Allowing for the confessional nature of her self-indictment and for the fact that it is, in effect, popular journalism, it is plain that Sara has enjoyed life looking after her poor mannies, as she calls them. Even Wilcher, though he suffers more because he is more sensitive than Sara, more concerned with what people think of him than Gulley and, more importantly, tormented by the idea of being other than he is, nevertheless succeeds to a quite considerable extent in satisfying the demands of his nature, and enjoys as much happiness as that nature permits. In this sense, all these characters, in spite of their misfortunes, are successes. Interestingly though, their success does not depend upon their having been educated for life. Thus Sara remarks at one point that even if her mother, who was a good, careful one, had still been alive, she would not have been able to influence her. Gulley's upbringing is powerless to influence him, in spite of the fact that it actually prevented him from wanting to become an artist, and the same is true of Wilcher's. He was brought up as a radical liberal and tried to convince himself that he was one, but in vain. Education for life is, after all, Cary seems to have decided, ineffectual in the face of the fixed in nature when it runs counter to it. Certainly, success in this second group of novels, clearly depends upon, first, the energy, persistence and ingenuity with which one's ends are pursued (Edward, Wilcher's elder brother, is an example of what happens when these fail), and, second, the ability to stay alive. Like Charley, Sara and Gulley are sent to prison, and Wilcher deserves to be, both as a molester of young women and as an arsonist, but whereas Charley's story terminates with his defeat, theirs continue and show that the only true defeat, provided that will and energy do not fail, is death.

The themes of the First Trilogy are twofold. First, Cary is exploring the implications of the three basic instincts his protagonists represent. Though these instincts rarely, if ever, exist in such pure form in life as in Cary's art – one does not expect to meet a Gulley Jimson in life as one might expect to meet, say, one of Jane Austen's people – nevertheless the characters embody aspects of the truth of human nature that one recognises and can respond to, provided that one realises that they are what they are and does not

try to react to them as if they were real human beings with the
potential for disinterested moral conduct. It is important also to
bear clearly in mind that Cary, in this trilogy and in the other two
books in the second group, is not discussing the question of how
man should live, but is demonstrating how, in his view, man does
live by responding to his given character of feeling.

Second, Cary is exploring the relationships between his concept
of woman and two basic conceptions of man, the conserver and
the creator. Sara tries to subdue them both to her purpose, and in
their different ways they both elude her. The situation here is
reminiscent of that in Shaw's *Man and Superman*, save that in
Cary's view man does not inevitably fall victim. If his own purposes are strong enough then they prevail and the woman is
thwarted. These relationships are worked out in terms of the
conflict of wills that Cary saw both as one of the sources of evil in
the world and as an inescapable condition of human existence.

Sara Monday's book, *Herself Surprised*, is thus essentially a
matter of variations on the theme of nest building and mothering.
In order to be true to his character, Cary had to limit her awareness of the world around her and so limit her possibilities as a
central figure around whom to construct a novel. The voice with
which she speaks is authentic and her narrative never flags, but
her book is necessarily the shortest and, in my view, the slightest
of the trilogy. It throws light upon Wilcher and Gulley Jimson and
prepares the way for their much weightier contributions, but not
to the point of being an essential introduction. Its part in the
unfolding of Cary's vision is to give the first fully developed
picture of his view of the essential nature of woman – all his female
characters from Sara on share her need to build nests and be
mothers – and to be the first major statement of the extent to
which the fixed in man's nature controls his destiny. Monday,
Hickson, Gulley and Wilcher, so very different from each other,
are all alike to her. One after the other, and two at a time when the
need and the opportunity arise, she takes them to her ample
bosom and lavishes herself upon them without stint. She is wife,
mistress, mother, servant, whatever the need, real or supposed, of
the individual or the moment may be. She makes a man of
Monday and makes this the justification of her adultery with
Hickson: 'he did me great services, and was a good friend . . . and
if I did wrong with Mr. Hickson so often, I can't believe but what I
did right' (*HS*, p. 37). Her role in life is to satisfy herself by

satisfying men. Conventional morality does not touch her, for all her lip-service to it.

In her management of Monday she is perfectly successful, his need of her, and of Hickson too, being so great that he refuses to see the truth about their relationship. But with Gulley and Wilcher she meets her match. Gulley is very willing to use women but totally unwilling to serve them. The struggle for mastery between him and Sara, for such it is, as Cary's use of Blake's 'The Mental Traveller' in *The Horse's Mouth* indicates, brings victory to neither. Sara cannot turn him into a respectable, portrait-painting husband with a good income derived from a series of satisfied sitters. He cannot turn her, as he does Nina and Lizzie, into a meek admirer of his genius who thinks it a privilege to serve him. The elemental woman and the artist are so evenly matched that Gulley, having inflicted a limited defeat on Sara by punching her on the nose, is obliged to break off the encounter and retreat himself.

Sara's relationship with Wilcher, though much less obviously a struggle, ends in defeat for her. Wilcher, like Gulley, is not a marrying man and like him again seeks to exploit women for his own purposes, as his book *To Be a Pilgrim* amply confirms. His attempts to marry Sara are both forced on to him by events he cannot control. Only when he is in danger of being dominated by Blanche, his niece, does he turn to Sara as the only available means of escape. He is also influenced by one of the periodic fits of guilt caused by his own awareness of the way in which he always seeks his own advantage. Therefore, even though we are told by Sara that he is busy making a settlement when she is arrested on the day before their wedding, it is hard to take him seriously as a would-be husband. He is saved by Blanche, apparently acting upon her own initiative, but since at the end of his life he recognises that he was incapable of behaving other than in accordance with his nature the reasonable supposition must be that he would have found some reason for withdrawing had that been necessary.

His second attempt to marry Sara, in *To Be a Pilgrim*, is also prompted by the need to escape from an intolerable situation. This time he is left alone by Ann with only hired servants to look after him, and becomes convinced that she will not return. Not surprisingly, the recurring delusion that he must be a pilgrim and move on comes to him again and under this pretext – it is real to him of course – he turns to Sara once again. But the Craven Gardens fire, on which his first proposal followed closely is now some four years in the past and Sara, whom at the beginning of the book, one month after her arrest, he proclaimed himself still anxious to marry, must have been out of prison for at least two years, and more if it is assumed that she received remission for good conduct. It is clear enough that once again he is motivated only by the desire to extricate himself from an unacceptable situation and to provide himself with another servant to replace Ann. But this time Sara is already well provided for, besides being in the awkward position of being in possession (rather improbably in fact) of furniture and other objects from the Craven Gardens house. There is, besides, no way in which she can use him for either her own or Fred's benefit, so, having no possible use for Wilcher she naturally turns him away.

The effect of these encounters is to underline Cary's basic assertion that man is the slave of his nature. The three characters only value each other in so far as they can use each other for their own ends. When they cannot, they reject each other. They never behave with disinterested goodwill. Cary's world is a tough one indeed.

The point is most fully developed in *To Be a Pilgrim*. Unlike Sara and Gulley, Wilcher, though a nonentity in it, moves in the world of affairs. By his own account, he understands very little of it: not the nature of things, nor his own nature, nor the natures of those around him. He blunders through life, perplexed and often mistaken, earnestly trying to discover what it is all about and how to cope. Like Cary himself, he has a dual nature. What he wants to be is in direct contrast to what he is, just as what Cary consciously thought is often in direct contrast to what he wrote in his novels. In his efforts to defy his own nature, he is Cary's most complex creation and his most interesting. In his political aspect, he epitomises the constant struggle between tradition and reform; in his sexual aspect, that between propriety and licence; and, in his family aspect, that between the need for a stable background and the need to go one's own way. But because in the end he remains true to his own given nature, he is also Cary's most convincing demonstration of the very limited nature of man's freedom. At the end of his life he finally attains the knowledge that the novelist has had all along: that the permanent aspects of nature cannot be overridden. He was not free to be a wanderer after all. Possessions are to him what the child is to its mother and act upon him with what was, to Cary, the same irresistible force.

The key to Wilcher's character is in the sentences: 'The love of possessions. It is spoken for a reproach and I feel it like a shame' (*TBP*, pp. 219–20). What is natural to him is culpable to society and it is this, plus the fact that, unlike Gulley, he has neither the courage nor the strength of character to go directly and openly for what he wants, that causes him to attempt to deny his own nature and pretend a liberalism and a love of religion that are not really in him. His political rantings at the election and his dressing up in Indian costume are merely his attempt to convince himself. It is always the insecure convert who makes the most noise and falls soonest by the wayside. His whole life is the action of a weak but stubborn character to achieve its purpose and at the same time justify itself to the world. It is clear, however, that he deceives none of his family and only partially deceives himself. He is a figure of pathos whose final confession is moving in spite of the fact that he is in many ways despicable. This confession is also an assertion of success in terms of his given nature. Regardless of the subterfuges and self-deceits he has felt obliged to resort to to conceal it, he has triumphantly pursued the search for satisfaction, just as Cary, in his novels, and like Wilcher at the point of death, triumphantly expressed his true vision.

He and his brothers and sister, taken together, may fairly be seen to approximate to a cross-section of radical upper-middle-class society of the early part of the twentieth century. Edward embodies the unusual and, as it turns out, unsuccessful combination of politics and the avant-garde arts. Bill represents the simple and unselfish response to life and duty that Cary admires in 'A Policy for Aid'; Lucy represents the nonconformist, evangelical approach to religion that tended to accompany Liberal political views; and Wilcher stands for law, finance and the natural conservatism that prevents liberals from becoming socialists. Of the three men, Edward may be regarded as the left, Bill the centre and Wilcher the right of the lay approach to life they collectively embody, whilst Edward the cynic and Lucy the evangelical Christian represent the religious extremes, with Wilcher occupying the centre ground. Amy, Bill's wife, forms a fifth member of the group, and embodies a simple, elemental, almost entirely instinctive response to life that both extends what her husband stands for and acts as a yardstick against which the others are measured. The organisation of the book is thus very tight, and Wilcher himself is by no means the only type-character in it.

Because the characters are types, they do not change. Lucy the child and Lucy the woman, for example, are identical, except in age. If one compares her with, say, Pip, in Dickens's _Great Expectations_, the point is very obvious. In Pip, the boy is superseded by the man and the change occurs as the result of a demonstrable process of maturation in response to experience. In Lucy, the girl merely acquires an adult body and the power to satisfy her nature in her own way. Finding herself in a rather similar position to Hedda Gabler, in possession of energies (not identical with Hedda's, of course) for which society makes no provision, she seizes the only opportunity that offers and goes off to lead the most adventurous and demanding life she can find. Her elopement with Brown is later echoed in _A Fearful Joy_ by the young Tabitha's cry, 'Oh-oh-oh, if only something would happen!' (_FJ_, p. 13) and the advent of Bonser.

A single illustration will perhaps suffice to establish the point. One of her major characteristics is her will to dominate. At the age of twelve though, significantly, 'already a woman in all the essentials of her craft and strategy' (_TBP_, p. 42), she challenges her father for supremacy. Having been beaten once during the day, she refuses to come to prayers.

> This, of course, was a direct challenge to my father and all of us understood very well that he would not care to beat her twice in the same day. That such a beating might have severe consequences for Lucy and therefore for him and all of us. And that Lucy was counting precisely on that point to defeat him (_TBP_, p. 43)

She fails, but is in no way affected by the experience: 'In fact, she never showed the smallest ill-effect of this nervous crisis' (_TBP_, p. 46). Years later, on the occasion of her first return home from Brown we find her dominating him as she packs to go back with him, and are told by Wilcher:

> as I learnt at a later time from one who had been a Benjamite, Lucy was a terror to Brown; she treated him often with such cruel and bitter contempt he would howl to be delivered from her. She had brought him publicly to tears on more than one occasion (_TBP_, p. 97)

As the child, so the woman. The success and failure are incidental: the will to dominate is constant.

It is true, of course, that Lucy returns to Brown at his command, but since he is her sole means of satisfaction, she can no more resist going back than going in the first instance. In any case, the same informant tells Wilcher that Brown did not want her back: 'It was God's command . . . I have been told he wrestled many days on his knees before he submitted, and I think we can see what God meant. For your sister was a great power – she gave him strength' (*TBP*, p. 97).

A point important for the understanding of Cary's world emerges here. Lucy gives Brown strength. We are told no more than that, but it is clear that Brown regards her as sent by God for this purpose, and himself as submitting to God's will in fetching her. The informed reader, however, knows that this cannot be so, because God cannot intervene in Cary's world. All that is happening is that the characters, who do not share Cary's insights (if they did, they could not hold the religious views that they do), are convinced that He both can intervene and does, and use this 'fact' to explain and justify their own actions. Lucy's effect upon Brown must therefore be seen as coincidental. She is merely acting so as to satisfy herself, for there is nowhere any indication that she regards herself as an inspiration to Brown or sets out to be one. She regards Brown as a representative of God because she can at one and the same time use him to satisfy her need to dominate and justify herself by claiming to be doing God's will in obeying him. She appeals over the heads of men to God for justification, and in order to obtain it she pays the heavy price of her life with the Benjamites, whom she hates and despises: 'If you knew what a set they are, Tommy. The mean jealousies and dirty little spites that creep about in them like worms in a dead rabbit' (*TBP*, p. 88). She thus occupies an intermediate position in the search for salvation between that occupied by Aissa, who was successful only at the price of death, and Syson, in *The Captive and the Free*, who achieves it as fully as it is possible for man to do. Lucy's achievement is incomplete because she has to pay continuously the price of submission to Brown, a price that is too heavy to be borne, hence her interludes at Tolbrook. She cannot have more salvation than she can afford to pay for. Her failure to achieve a permanent state of salvation arises from the fact that, unlike Aissa and Syson, she is unable to approach God directly. She needs Brown, accepting him as both master and medium, but, as Marshall McLuhan pointed out, the medium is the message, and Brown is not God. We thus have a paradoxical situation in which he at once facilitates and prevents the achievement of salvation by Lucy. Cary's Protestant background is evident at this point.

Brown, who is likewise intent upon self-satisfaction, is in a similar position and bears with Lucy because on balance the benefits of association with her outweigh the drawbacks. He is able to make use of her almost as one uses a stream of water to produce electricity. He taps her energy and converts it to a form he can use for his own purposes. This, incidentally, is why Cary is fascinated by energy: not for its own sake as Lord David Cecil has suggested,[8] but because nothing worthwhile can be done without it. His world operates like the world of Nature. Everything is part of a giant chain-reaction, reminiscent of the medieval Chain of Being. Apparently disconnected phenomena are essential to each other; all entities thrive by exploiting each other in some way, seeking their own ends, but giving and receiving help in the process, their success or failure depending upon the maintenance of a precarious balance of Nature. Man alone is conscious of the process and is able to rationalise it in terms flattering to himself, a point underlined by Wilcher's indecent exposure of himself. Other reasons for it may, of course, be fairly imputed, but this is the reason he himself gives: 'To wake her [the girl] up. To excite her. To make something happen, for myself as well as for her' (*TBP*, p. 306). His rational mind is horrified, but at the same time he is excited and fascinated by what he is doing: 'as my adventures became more bold and more scandalous, so the loathing and the triumph increased' (*TBP*, p. 307). Basically, what is happening is that Wilcher is taking part, in the only way he can at this point, in the same process of interaction that is exemplified by Brown's and Lucy's need for each other. His action is a perverted one, certainly, but there are plenty of precedents in Nature for that, and Wilcher's conduct is to be seen as an aberration of one of the fundamental processes of Cary's world. He is trying, unsuccessfully, to function as a Carian spellbinder.

This life-giving function of energy in the novels may be compared directly with Cary's views on the function of the novelist as he expressed them in his articles 'The Function of the Novel'[9] and 'What Does Art Create?'[10] In the former he maintained that the essential function of the artist lies not in forming his idea of the world, since that is something all men do, but in communicating it; whilst in the latter he asserted that the essential effect of art is to create new life. Creation is thus depicted as the effect of the successful carrying out of his natural function by the artist: it is an end-product, not a prime force. So it is with Brown and Lucy. The life that they create arises not from some mysterious source within themselves but as the result of each of them responding fully to the demands of his own nature and interacting with the other in the process. The status of creativity is no doubt diminished by this way of regarding it, but its existence and nature are plausibly accounted for, so far as the account goes.

Edward reinforces Cary's message by representing the other side of the coin, for he is used to show how failure arises when the demands of nature are not complied with. At the beginning of his political career he makes a remark that proves to be prophetic:

> 'One thing at any rate is certain. I'll never do much in politics.'
> 'Now why on earth should you say that when you've already had such a success?'
> 'Anyone can make a beginning in politics – it's the finish that kills' (*TBP*, p. 70)

This is Cary's way of indicating not only that Edward does not have the makings of a successful politician in him but also that there is nothing to be done about it. Edward lacks Brown's and Lucy's (and Nimmo's) unshakable conviction of the rightness of his actions and is consequently a cynic, as many of his couplets indicate:

> I [Wilcher] was shocked and disgusted when Edward, after a meeting in which his eloquence had brought tears to our eyes, passed me this scrap of paper:
>
> > Let tyrannies all to free republics pass
> > The one by coppers ruled; the others, brass (*TBP*, p. 154)

Edward's true vocation is that of Waster, in the medieval sense, and connoisseur of modern art; and his failure stems from the fact that he follows another career, that of politics, in spite of his conviction that it is not for him. The explanation of this is to be found in the early environmental factor that Cary attached so much importance to, and to the fact that Edward is the victim of family tradition. We are not told explicitly why he takes to politics, but Wilcher is made to say that 'Edward, like his grandfather, became member for Queensport' (*TBP*, p. 69). We must therefore see Edward as one who, like Aladai, failed in life because he has the wrong sort of education and is thus prevented from seeking the satisfaction that is proper to him. The subconscious knowledge of this would certainly account for his virtual withdrawal from political life as a result of losing his seat, and for his refusal to accept the seat that is subsequently offered to him. Clearly, he is not a political animal. It would also render plausible the fact that his eventual attempt to return to politics is made only at the instigation of his second wife. He has been misdirected by force of circumstances, has no one to salvage him, and lacks both the energy and the knowledge of 'the nature of things' necessary to put himself right.

This again underlines the importance of energy in Cary's world. It is not merely desirable but vital that man responds to the natural drive that is in him if the essential chain reaction is to take place. It also defines the nature of the concept. Energy in Cary's world is not mere activity, but a force essential to purposeful activity in pursuit of satisfaction. Thus Edward, for all his violence on the hustings, is essentially lacking in true energy, perhaps better termed vitality. He could not resist misdirection, nor can he either re-activate or re-direct himself when failure comes in the shape of a lost election.

Evidence that he has been diverted from his true course and is of no real force as a statesman is to be found in the fact that in the only glimpse of him in action that is given, he is seen giving serious consideration to a scheme to replace the perfectly adequate Queensport Ferry with a more expensive light railway, because people expect new governments to make changes (*TBP*, p. 196). If we were meant to take him seriously, Cary could have done better than this, even though the necessity of novelty is one of his recurrent themes.[11] The ultimate failure is thus the failure of vitality, the failure to insist on being one's true self even though it leads to destruction. The direct and obvious contrast is with Gulley, who, in spite of being directed away from art by his early experience, finds himself as an artist and insists on pursuing his natural vocation against all odds. He has what Aladai and

Edward, especially, lack, and is the standard against which their failure is made apparent.

It is not, however, necessary to go outside *To Be a Pilgrim* in order to obtain a contrast, though of a somewhat different kind, to Edward. Amy is an outstanding example of an unconsciously successful Cary character. She has been allowed to develop unhindered in a sheltered environment and really is completely unspoilt and unsophisticated. She takes life as it comes because she knows nothing but what she experiences and does only what she wants, not because, like Lucy, she is wilful, but because she knows no other way of behaving. Because she has never had to re-direct herself on to the right lines, she has never had to realise herself, and, having none of the disadvantages and difficulties that Cary's characters normally have to contend with, represents the author's conception of human conduct in a pure form. Because she is a Cary woman, it is natural to Amy to find a man and bear children, and she surpasses all of her kind by agreeing to marry Bill at their first meeting, taking to the role of wife and mother like the proverbial duck to water and never allowing herself to be deflected from her purpose by anyone from the moment she enters the book to the moment of her death. At her first appearance, she is already quite fixed in her response to life. Wilcher says that 'Amy's own [distinct] life continued from the day of her marriage' (*TBP*, p. 111), and he goes on to relate how Amy, a girl of eighteen and bride of a few days, left alone in the house of her husband's family, seemingly without realising what she is doing, rejects her mother-in-law's opinion and her husband's known dislike of the colour and chooses blue for her bedspread in defiance of them both. For all her innocence, Amy cannot be deflected from her unconscious pursuit of self-satisfaction, so that Bill is making no understatement when at the end of his life he says to Wilcher: 'Fact is Amy doesn't want to do what I want to do. She's been the finest wife a chap could hope for, as you know, I couldn't have done without her. But there it is' (*TBP*, p. 261). In spite of her total inflexibility, Amy's life is highly successful because she fulfils the essential conditions for success in Cary's world: first, she responds fully to the demands of her nature; and second, she is in her correct niche, which is to say that her education and environment have reinforced her natural disposition and not, like Edward's, thwarted it. It is for these reasons that at the end of her life, living alone in one room at her own choice, she can say: 'I've been lucky – thirty years with Bill – and the boys, so much happiness' (*TBP*, p. 337). Amy, and Bill too, whom it is not necessary to discuss separately because they are so much of a kind, are idealised figures who have achieved the only form of paradise that Cary sees as being open to man: complete fulfilment in Blake's eternal now. In terms of worldly fame they are nonentities, but they play their little parts in the scheme of things to perfection and die content. More than that, in Cary's world, it is not possible for man to do, for fulfilment lies within.

The fulfilment which Bill and Amy achieve is indicated by their lack of interest in metaphysics. When Wilcher suggests to Amy that she will soon be seeing Bill again, she fails completely to respond: 'I said this for comfort to the poor woman, but her expression did not change. Like Bill himself, she seemed to take little concern in what happened after her death' (*TBP*, p. 337). If life is lived as it is meant to be, the question of the after-life becomes irrelevant, as it seems to have been to Cary himself, for, in spite of his unshakable belief in God, he had nothing whatever to say about it.

There can be little doubt that in eulogising Amy, Wilcher becomes Cary's direct mouthpiece:

> I don't know that Amy believed, but her faith did not need theology. Its strong roots were in a character which nothing could shake.
>
> When we laughed at Amy as a young bride, left alone in our household of clever young people, she withdrew into her pride. But she was brave by nature, and did not sulk in it. She used it only for her home and her refuge. For her pride was not vain; it was nothing more than the ordinary self-respect which all brave people have by nature. She set no great value on herself and so she had no self pity.
>
> And now lying here, I miss Amy more than all those I have known. I know why Amy sent away that curate and would not let me talk to her about the consolations of religion. She did not want them; perhaps she did not altogether like them. Perhaps in her shrewd mind, as simple and strong as Sara's, she was sceptical of heaven   (*TBP*, p. 339)

Cary's personal admiration for his character seems to shine through Wilcher's words, an impression that is heightened by the fact that Wilcher goes on to receive an insight that is for him an experience comparable to Cary's own experience when he realised the nature of things:

> To Amy, death . . . was a familiar, and she received him like an afternoon caller. But to me here death is a wonder. When I look now at the last horizon, I see him rise into the sky, more illuminating than the brightest sun, colder than the arctic moon; and all the landscape is suddenly altered. The solid hills melt into cloud; and clouds affirm a reality.
> Familiar shapes are changed before my eyes. And seeing these strange patterns, these immense shadows reaching to my feet, I say, 'I never knew this place before. I have lived like a mole in a run; like a cat in a kitchen' (*TBP*, p. 339)

Cary, after his initial insights, wrote quickly and easily. Wilcher, after his, dies quickly and easily. In realising at last his true nature, and in seeing that after all he has obeyed its dictates, he has achieved salvation. Change, as he acknowledges many times throughout the book, especially in relation to Robert's activities, is both inevitable and necessary, but conservation is no less so. If he had not preserved Tolbrook, Edward and Lucy would both have suffered for it, and so would their children, Ann and Robert, whose role it is to make the changes that the movement of history has made imperative. Progress does not, as Wilcher mistakenly thought, reside in individuals, but in generations. The conserver cannot become the reformer. His job is to play his part, in the knowledge that when it is time for him to be superseded, the reformer will appear. And when that time comes, he must accept it gracefully, as Amy accepted that she had played her role out when Bill died. The life that she and he had created in the form of the garden had to be handed on, and it is for this reason that she refuses Wilcher's offer of a loan to buy the freehold of the cottage and goes to look over the hedge to ensure that it is being well-used. In this respect too, she is an example to Wilcher.

This incident also illustrates the nature of the pilgrimage, the idea of which underlies the book. It is not a journey in search of something, for there is nowhere to go, nothing to seek. There is only what Wilcher himself describes as 'this broad day-time of eternity' (*TBP*, p. 341). He comes to realise, implicitly, that the wandering religious life, such as Lucy undertakes, is merely another way of life and as such no more admirable or desirable than any other. That is why, for all his love of Lucy during her lifetime, it is Amy that he misses most in the end. She, not Lucy, is the true pilgrim, for the pilgrim's goal is, ultimately, death and the true pilgrim is the man or woman who has learnt how to reach it gracefully. Edward is thus no pilgrim, for he dies embittered and unfulfilled; nor does Lucy achieve full pilgrim status, for her death is purely the result of her misguided stubbornness. Old Wilcher, the father, does. He recognises the need to move on and goes without repining: 'Too long in same camp' (*TBP*, p. 158). And finally, Wilcher himself does, for he learns to be content with having played out his role, and so learns how to die, and in doing so he becomes like Amy:

> What do I care about the other world? One dies and learns. Probably these young people who don't believe in Heaven are right   (*TBP*, p. 341)

> Material love. What is material? What is the body? Is not this house the house of spirits, made by generations of lovers?   (*TBP*, p. 342)

The influence of Blake is again apparent.

> . . . it was understood between us [him and Ann] that whether I die today or tomorrow does not matter to anybody. But for her that is a defeat; for me it is a triumph   (*TBP*, p. 342)

In this triumph lies the crowning irony of the book, for Wilcher has just confessed himself a failure as a pilgrim, not realising that by this very confession he has attained pilgrim's stature at last, and is ready to make the journey. The precise nature of the triumph lies in Wilcher's subconscious acceptance – it is Cary's also – of the fact that he is not free in any substantial way and not committed beyond this life. The awful burden of responsibility has been lifted from him, or rather has disappeared like the chimera that it is, and his earth has become his heaven.

Cary's use of Blake's vision of life, with which he was in profound sympathy, throughout *The Horse's Mouth* indicates that Gulley is in a similar state of being. In the world's eyes he is a miserable failure, a dirty, dishonest, semi-vagrant who once painted a few good pictures. But in his own terms he enjoys a very large measure of success. He succeeds in being an artist from the time his true nature manifests itself to his death, and, with the one exception of the 'forgery' which he sells to the Beeders, he paints only what he wants to paint. The only limit to his success is his lack of money for materials, which necessitates his wasting time acquiring it by whatever means he can when he wants to be painting. What the world calls morality and respectability are, as with Sara, irrelevant to Gulley, as is poverty. Where he differs from Sara, and all the other Cary protagonists, is that his understanding of the nature of things is crystal clear: it is, in fact, Cary's (the thinker's, not the novelist's) own. He knows exactly how the world sees him, and recognises that it cannot see him otherwise, because it, too, has its own nature to which it must respond. He knows, therefore, that government cannot be other than it is nor behave other than as it does. He knows that what is original in his work will not immediately be recognised because there are no standards existing by which to judge it. He knows that injustice is endemic and that anger is a self-damaging waste of time. The whole book is Cary's major demonstration of how the world works, and Gulley is his medium. He understands all, accepts all, and gets on with the job of fulfilling his own nature.

Full appreciation of the book, however, depends upon understanding the nature of Gulley as a character. He must be seen as allegorical. The idea of taking Gulley as a credible representation of a real human being is absurd. Only when seen as a personification of the human instinct to try to come to terms with life via the creation of art does he make sense. The difficulty, of course, is that this kind of characterisation is so rare in the novel, so completely unexpected, that it is easy not to recognise it and to regard Gulley as an attempt at the creation of an artist that has been carried to such extremes of exaggeration as to be unsuccessful. But Gulley is kin to Sir Epicure Mammon, Volpone and all the others of that large and honourable family, and behaves accordingly. He is a certain aspect of the human character in action.

Where he differs from most of his peers is that the conduct he embodies is not being satirised. Nor, however, is the reader's sympathy being sought. There is no suggestion that Gulley represents the great artist suffering in the face of an uncomprehending, philistine society. The very question of whether or not his wall paintings have any value is nullified by their destruction and by the fact that his posthumous reputation is dependent on earlier work which he himself came to deprecate. The value of his work is irrelevant. What matters is that he is an original artist, trying to give effect to his personal vision of life (or rather, that is what he is meant to be, for Cary has weakened the effect by making him so very dependent on Blake for his ideas), and the author's purpose is to show, in quintessential form, the inevitable consequences of such a state of being, the problems and penalties that the successful attempt to respond fully to the demands of such a nature entail. But according to Cary, and the point is made very plainly in the book, every man has to use his imagination in his efforts to create for himself the world his nature demands, and so every man is an original creative artist, regardless of whether or not he produces art in the generally understood sense of the term. Gulley is therefore not merely an allegory of the artist, but an allegory of man. He is Mankind and his problems are particularised and intensified versions of ours. The difference between Gulley and us, the fact that enables him to fill this role, is that because he is not a 'real' human being, even in fictional terms, he is able to follow the demands of his nature with a single-mindedness that few, if any, human beings emulate – fortunately. Imagine a world of Gulleys! In practice, we moderate the demands of our natures for all kinds of reasons – personal affection and the consequent willingness to benefit others at our own expense, for example. Gulley does not. In practice, we are not blessed with inexhaustible energy. Gulley is. In practice, no matter how strong our beliefs about the nature of things and in what we are doing, we are subject to periods of doubt and despondency. Gulley is not. He is again 'the thing itself', unmodified human nature, and so exemplifies those deepest drives that in practice we usually try to temper or even disparage for one reason or another. He is thus the central figure of this phase of Cary's work, but he does not, of course, represent Cary's final vision, and it is regrettable that, because his book has caught readers' imaginations more than any other, it is so often assumed that he does.

Gulley's account of the way in which he became an artist against his will is the plainest statement in the whole of Cary's fiction of the importance he attached to the permanent in nature. It is not essential to the narrative even though it is made to serve the additional purpose of revealing more of Gulley's past life, but it is essential to the understanding of Cary's view of life and it is no accident that it occurs in this book, the climax of the trilogy. Here Cary makes the matter as explicit as it can be made without authorial interpolation, and in so doing reinforces what has been implicit in the earlier two books. The impossibility of communicating with God is also spelt out when Gulley is removing the fish from the Fall:

'They're dead. They don't swim – they don't speak, they don't click, they don't work, they don't do anything at all.'
 'But why don't they?'
 'God knows. But he won't go into details. The truth is, THE OLD HORSE DOESN'T SPEAK ONLY HORSE. And I can't speak only Greenbank.' (*HM*, p. 50)

The necessity of reliance upon oneself is clear. The nature of freedom is also clearly delineated during the interview between Coker and Hickson, when Gulley is led by his response to his own painting of Sara to criticise Spinoza: 'Contemplation, in fact, is ON THE OUTSIDE. . . . Freedom, to be plain, is nothing but the INSIDE OF THE OUTSIDE. And even a philosopher like old Ben can't judge the XXX by eating pint pots' (*HM*, p. 103). The free man drinks the beer, plunges into life. He doesn't sit looking at it. Freedom resides in active involvement, not in passive contemplation. 'But what you get on the inside . . . is the works – it's SOMETHING THAT GOES ON GOING ON. . . . It's the ginger in the gingerbread. . . . It's the creation' (*HM*, p. 104). Freedom, that is, resides in the unceasing attempt to create one's own world, an activity that goes on as long as life endures and gives it its zest. Once again, there is no question choosing what that world is to be. There cannot be, and one achieves freedom by making the response to whatever happens to be inside. This is brought out clearly in Gulley's comparison of Sara with Rozzie when he and Sara meet at Rozzie's grave. She, like Edward Wilcher, is one of those characters who lack vitality, for all her fierce exterior. Whereas Sara, intent on her own purposes, had to be fought off, Rozzie had to be looked after. 'You loved her like a ruin that has to be propped up and railed round to keep the dogs off' (*HM*, p. 259). The thought is Gulley's and Sara does not agree with him, but when it is remembered that it was Rozzie who could not bring herself to take the hotel at

Brighton (in *Herself Surprised*), who does nothing at all with her life after her husband's death, and who lets herself be taken at will by Gulley, it is clear that his judgement is right. She is passive; for whatever the reason (no indication is given) she has no purpose in life, and she is not free.

More than that, she despairs, gives up on life, and it is this that constitutes the essence of her attraction for Gulley and gives rise to the reflection I have just quoted. It is the attraction of decadence, of decay, of opting out. Gulley feels it and cannot entirely resist it. It even brings out in him a streak of domesticity that is totally uncharacteristic as he struggles (*HM*, p. 256) to make up for Rozzie's total inadequacy as a mother, the ultimate sign of failure in a Cary woman. Her attraction is so strong precisely because, for Gulley, the fight for freedom is so hard. The horse's voice, the permanent in his nature, drives him relentlessly, and so much so that he would be glad to give up if he could. This aspect of Gulley is foreshadowed in *Herself Surprised* when his then 'wife' Nina says, in response to Sara's question: why does he paint like that? 'It's the only way he can paint. But I sometimes think he would like to stop' (*HS*, p. 58). It is underlined throughout the book by the whole series of derogatory remarks that he makes about himself and about artists. He says, for example, that when he was a respectable clerk he enjoyed life (*HM*, p. 61); he is glad that his son Tommy has no wish to become an artist; and he does his best to deter Nosy Barbon. There is no reason to doubt his sincerity. The comedy is a front: it is really a hell of a life, as well as being a heaven. The one is the price that must be paid for the other. The point is made clearly in what Gulley says to Nosy when they are walking along Greenbank in the rain. If man wants heaven he can have it, but he must make it for himself by dint of endless toil. If he doesn't work 'he just tumbles about in hell' (*HM*, p. 74). Heaven must be sweated for, hence the attraction of Rozzie, even to so absolute a servant of the horse as Gulley.

With him, of course, the horse's voice is always the stronger, and part of the price he has to pay for his heaven, his fulfilment of himself as a painter, is his knowledge of man's essential alone-ness. Again, the point is made in conversation with Nosy, this time when they are fleeing from the fiasco in the Beeders' flat, in the passage beginning: 'One man is a living soul, but two men are an indiarubber milking machine for a beer engine . . .' (*HM*, p. 218). The bigger the group, the more harm it does. 'After all,

what is a people? It doesn't exist. Only individuals exist – . . .'
(*HM*, p. 220), and nothing can bring them together. It is not a new
idea; none of Cary's is; but Gulley's forceful expression of it
underlines the sombre nature of man's existence in a world in
which a further part of the price that must be paid for heaven is the
hell of isolation as he struggles to respond to the voice of his own
particular horse. No one can help him, and he must exploit his
fellows for his own ends ruthlessly, as Gulley does, if he is to have
any chance of success – and the greater the success he achieves,
the greater his suffering will be. Gulley makes fun of himself and
light of his knavery with tongue-in-cheek naïvety. He has to, or he
could not do the things he does, and as his suffering increases he
laughs the more loudly. His laughter is an indicator of his pain
and a reminder that he also represents suffering mankind.

The fact that from time to time Gulley's humour degenerates
into facetiousness and his mock-innocence sometimes grates is to
be accounted for and is put into perspective by the self-defensive
nature of his bravado. It is also necessary to remember that, like
all storytellers, Gulley exaggerates. His narrative must be seen as
a ball bouncing on a jet of water above the level of the pond itself,
which is never seen. Nevertheless, it is there, and it is that, the
pond from which the jet of water comes, that constitutes the
reality of the events that underlie the highly coloured ball that
Gulley beguiles himself with as well as his audience.

This aspect of the book is best illustrated by reference to the flat
episode. Abel, even by comparison with Gulley, is outrageous; so
much so that Gulley alongside him seems almost normal. The
technique he is being made to use here is that of parody, his
subject is himself and Abel is his vehicle. Clear indication that this
is what is happening is given at the outset. The Beeders' flat is in
the attic of a large building, yet we are told that a four-ton block of
stone is swung through its windows by means of what must have
been a very large crane indeed, and expected to believe that
during both this operation and the protracted and noisy process of
carving it, not to mention the removal of the Beeders' possessions,
the porter never becomes aware of what is happening. And to cap
everything, the Beeders are supposed to have taken it all, like good
millionaires, with scarcely a quiver. We cannot be meant to take
this literally and it is readily apparent that the underlying reality
must have been something very much less ridiculous. Certainly
Gulley did occupy the flat and begin a mural. Certainly a sculptor

did do some work there. No doubt some of the Beeders' possessions were pawned. No doubt Gulley and others did play up to the
porter. But the whole incident can only have been a shadow of
that which Gulley describes. The fact that it happened at all and
that Gulley and his friends escaped the consequences is sufficient
evidence of this.

What happens here, I think, is that Gulley, the compulsive
artist, one part of whom would be glad to stop, indulges in a
fantasy whose ultimate purpose is to reassure himself and persuade his readers that he is perhaps not so very outrageous after
all. The comedy of Gulley's already highly-coloured account of
his activities rises at this point to farce, and the episode is therefore
the outward expression of his most painful realisation of his own
plight and Cary's of the unrelieved human lot.

The book is given coherence by the three paintings that Gulley
is involved with: the Fall, the resurrection (not of Jesus but of
Lazarus–man) and the Creation, and the three together form the
fable that underlies it. Cary's basic point – man's need to respond
creatively to life – is clear enough, and is in any case spelt out by
Gulley in the conversation with Nosy already referred to, when
he talks about man's fall into freedom. It is the paucity of the
actual freedom in contrast with the grandiosity of the idea that
ultimately gives the book its force and Gulley his pathos.

THE MOONLIGHT

The remaining two books in this group add nothing essential to
the picture given in the First Trilogy. We know, because Cary
makes it perfectly clear in the preface to the Carfax edition, that
The Moonlight was written to promulgate his view of the nature of
women, to 'give the true case for women as a sex, the real dilemma
of a girl who is held by nature in so firm a grip' (*TM*, p. 10). The
grip is that of the necessity of breeding, and it constitutes another
version of the horse's mouth. Amanda should not be seen as an
individual in whom the impulse to breed happens to be irresistibly
strong. She is intended to be Everywoman, mid-twentieth century
style, for Cary was convinced that all women are intended to be
mothers and that their major role in life is to bear children and
rear them. The preface makes this clear. He admires the Victorian

age because 'it concentrated . . . on woman's central importance to family life' (*TM*, p. 6), dismisses the twenties because it was a time 'when college girls were told that it was a crime against their sex in its battle for freedom, to have any children at all' (*TM*, pp. 7–8), and praises modern women for choosing both children and careers.

Cary's assumption that motherhood is a 'fundamental and eternal character of being', is certainly true, but whether or not it is as great a force in the average woman's life as he supposed is open to argument. We cannot be sure to just what extent motherhood is an involuntary activity until all women are completely free to reject it if they wish, and all other things are equal. For this reason the point may never be settled, and to the extent that Cary's view of woman is too sweeping, the women in *The Moonlight* must be regarded as type-characters who represent a certain kind of woman, the mother, rather than Woman as an entity. This in no way invalidates the book, of course, but it does mean that it does not possess the universal significance that Cary intended it to have.

Cary's conviction of the firmness of nature's grip on women underlines once again the very limited nature of his concept of freedom. The compulsive mother is not free to choose to have children and her power to do what she likes is restricted to choosing what seems to be the best way of doing what she must. Rose, because of the pressure of circumstances and her sense of duty, makes her sisters and even her father her children. Bessie is made to take Rose's place with James Groom, so that the family life she produces is a vicarious fulfilment for Rose as well as a direct fulfilment for herself. This is made clear by Ella's reflection: 'Yes, Bessie and Rose invented James's greatness. But why did Bessie always pretend she had loved James from the beginning? She didn't really believe it herself. It was a kind of idea' (*TM*, p. 101). Ella, thwarted in her wish to marry, nevertheless manages to produce a child, and, such is the strength of the fecundity embodied in her, succeeds in manoeuvring her daughter into doing the same. Amanda herself goes to the ditch with Harry in an almost trance-like state, mildly amazed at what she is doing, but quite unable to resist. There can be no doubt that these are just as much type-characters as Gulley, Sara and Wilcher.

Given these limits, however, the book, in spite of the hothouse intensity that the concentration on the pursuit of motherhood generates, is a success. The four women form a quartet and together play out Cary's theme. Rose is dominated by Victorian propriety and a strong sense of duty. She resolutely stands aside from marriage and arranges for Bessie to take her place, but retains Ella in particular as a surrogate child who, in the absence of an acceptable suitor, must be protected against the ineligible Ernest Cranage. When her measures fail and Ella elopes with him, then it becomes her duty to protect Amanda, Ella's illegitimate child, from the knowledge and the consequences of her mother's action. By treating her sister as the irresponsible child she in some ways is, Rose gives such satisfaction as she can to the permanent in her nature.

Bessie is an obvious variant of Sara. She takes Rose's place readily enough, but a husband and a large family cannot satisfy her either, and she indulges in a series of lovers to give her nature the satisfaction it needs. Her effortless success in managing husband, lovers and children make her the least interesting of the three sisters.

Ella is the most complex, because she is torn between her upbringing, which has given her a sincerely held belief in the Victorian ideal of marriage (witness her statement that Rose was right to separate her from Cranage and their child), and her nature as a Cary-woman, which over-rules her education and compels her to behave in what is by the standards of her time an abandoned manner. In her conduct, one notes once again how Cary's early concern with education gives way before the power of nature, especially as her concern with marriage and motherhood does not stop with herself but is projected on to her daughter, whom she is determined to marry to Harry Dawbarn at all costs, even to the extent of 'losing' Rose's will so that the money to set them up in a farm will be forthcoming. Her reason is powerless to resist the commands that emanate from the horse's mouth, whose servant she too is. Education can help in carrying out those commands, but it cannot change the message.

Amanda is her mother again in the changed context of the mid-twentieth century. She is more intelligent and much better educated and she has her generation's ideas about liberation: for her, marriage is by no means the only career, and it is not a state she wishes to enter into. But her feminine instincts assert themselves in the form of a shocked realisation of her own sexuality. The significance that the Victorian dressmaker's dummy has for her accounts for the horror she feels at the sight of her own leg (*TM*, p. 150) as she discovers that she and the dummy are akin. It represents the Victorian male's view of woman as an alluring sexual object; the shock that Amanda experiences arises from her realisation that it is not the male alone who knows sexual desire and that she cannot remain aloof. The incident is reminiscent of Gulley's discovery that he has to be an artist. But although she submits to Harry's embrace and becomes pregnant, she is able to resist marriage, which her world does not absolutely demand. In her case, education, whilst not able to nullify the horse's commands, is able to modify the consequences of obeying. The child conceived, she can dispense with the father.

Essentially, then, *The Moonlight* is a study of how four women in different though related circumstances cope with the demands of the common element in their natures. 'Variations on a theme' might have been a better title.

A FEARFUL JOY

Cary's final exploration of his concept of an unchanging response in an ever-changing situation occurs in *A Fearful Joy*. His portrayal in it of the historical scene, however, such as it is, is not of any particular interest in itself. It serves rather the function of a necessary backcloth against which the characters play out their parts than that of a vital force with which they are obliged to interact in their struggle to fulfil themselves. The central figure, Tabitha, is delineated in the first few short chapters of the book, and is shown growing up in a late-Victorian world. At fourteen 'she was still remarkable for nothing but a certain violence of ordinariness' (*FJ*, p. 10), but at fifteen she develops rather a straightlaced attitude to life and a disposition to impose her views upon others:

grasping for the first time in her life an idea of conduct, she entered with fervour, characteristically a little too much fervour, upon its realisation. She became a good deal of a prig, a prude. She went to church on saints' days. At seventeen, as a prefect, she made war upon the silly and the weak. She even

> denounced bicycles, discovering how wide a door they opened
> to vicious curiosity and evil freedoms   (*FJ*, p. 12)

in spite of having been overjoyed at being given one by her father.
But as always her need for self-satisfaction is stronger than any
imagined moral scruples:

> For six months Tabitha was firmly resolved to be a mission-
> ary. . . . But this ambition was suddenly destroyed by the
> arrival of a missionary to stay at the Cedars, for though he was a
> hero he was also very severe on the modern girl. The sight of a
> girl on a bicycle caused him horror and misery . . .
>   Tabitha, in spite of her austere views on female conduct,
> instantly detested anyone who should dare to criticise her sex or
> attempt to deprive them of any of the new liberties. She retorted
> upon the visitor that she herself rode a bicycle and why
> not?   (*FJ*, p. 13)

Like all Cary's characters, she is indifferent to moral standards as
soon as they threaten to become restrictive. The options must be
kept open so that the most expedient choice can always be made,
hence the sudden change of ground when her liberty is
threatened.

This disposition to vehemence both in attitude and action,
however, is not accompanied by any consciousness of her true
purpose. She determines to become a concert pianist and prac-
tises six hours a day for over a year, but:

> She herself was often seized with restlessness, with a strange
> horror for the piano and even for her own beloved room. It was
> in such a fit one day that, leaning her nose and forehead on the
> window and gazing at, but not seeing, the spring blossom in the
> front garden below, she cried out, startling herself, 'Oh-oh-oh,
> if only something would happen!'   (*FJ*, p. 13)

What happens is Bonser, and it is her elopement with him and the
resulting pregnancy that reveals her as a Cary woman, responding to what, according to Cary, is permanent in her nature.

> She murmurs at night to the dark, 'But it's absolute madness.
> How can I run off with a man?'

> Yet she knows perfectly well that whatever Bonser is (and she is only half deceived) she is going to run off with him. She can no more withdraw from that adventure than a young boy who has climbed up a high springboard can refuse to dive (*FJ*, p. 19)

Or, one might add, than a Gulley Jimson can refuse to paint. Tabitha is clearly not determining her own purpose. She is as much in the grip of the Life Force as Shaw's Ann Whitfield and, having got herself pregnant against Bonser's wishes, she tries to secure him as a permanent occupant of her nest, only to repeat Sara's experience with Gulley in receiving a bloody nose.

At this point Tabitha's character is fully established and it does not change. Her Carian indifference to independent moral standards in the face of necessity reappears when her indignant rejection of Jobson's offer on behalf of Sturge is quickly followed by her ready acceptance when her only alternative, a return home to her brother Harry and his offensive wife Edith, proves to be even less desirable. It is noticeable that she at no time reproaches herself, nor is she ever portrayed as a victim to be pitied. Once her most expedient course of action is clear to her, she pursues it calmly and resolutely, getting her own way as much as she possibly can, and giving only as much as is necessary to get it. She takes Sturge to her bed with terrifying thoroughness more than three months after her installation in the flat when it becomes clear that she can maintain her own position and so secure her son's in no other way.

Unlike Sara's, Tabitha's talent for nest building extends beyond mothering men. She is an able hostess and has the ability to manage people too, and the success of 'The Banksider' is largely hers. She includes all the men involved in it in her activities and keeps the various opposing forces in balance with considerable success. Once again, however, she is not a prime mover. She is Manklow's mouthpiece and furthers his ideas consistently, thus, in effect, paying off her debt to him for services rendered. She is probably not conscious of this; at any rate, there is no indication of it. The point is that Manklow has his finger on the pulse of the times, he knows what will sell, and Tabitha always needs to be animated by somebody else's ideas before she can function. She thus uses Manklow for her own purposes, both in providing Sturge with the value for money he needs as a patron of the arts if he is to continue to maintain her, and in satisfying the needs of her own nature for what constitutes, in her own eyes, a moral purpose and an outlet for her inherent disposition to vehement action. This is apparent in her refusal of the offer of marriage she receives when on holiday in order to return to the exciting and stimulating 'Banksider' situation.

The next phase of Tabitha's life, her marriage to Gollan, is simply a variation of the Sturge phase. It is preceded by another unsuccessful return home; is instigated by Gollan and accepted by her after initial rejection. This time, however, the fact of expediency is touched by Cary with comic irony. Having decided to accept Gollan only after she has ascertained that she will not be required to pretend to be in love with him and that her son will be welcome, 'It is with the sense of performing a moral act that she says firmly, "If you're quite sure, Sir James" ' (*FJ*, p. 148). Her main purpose secured, Tabitha sets out to satisfy Gollan as she satisfied Sturge, and, as the two men are very different, so the method she adopts is different. Sturge was essentially a weak man who did not know how to obtain what he wanted and had to have success forced upon him. Gollan knows precisely how to get what he wants and will brook no interference. He is apologetic when Tabitha tries to control him but not deterred, and keeps disappearing on lengthy errands:

> Tabitha, in spite of her irritation, perceives that she has been naive, . . . And when Gollan comes at last, full of apologies, she looks at him with respect as well as irritation. She thinks, 'Yes, I've been silly. You can see what a will he has; he's just been teaching me.' And in the thought she feels, unexpectedly, with all her annoyance, a certain comfort   (*FJ*, p. 153)

Her end is achieved, for the foreseeable future at least, and she can afford to relax.

It is not necessary to follow Tabitha all through the book since her conduct is entirely consistent, which fact is in itself consistent with her type-character status. At the end of the book, when, finally alone and apparently defeated, she responds to the small, square child and prays that death may not come that day, she becomes the embodiment of the fierce will to live in spite of the worst that life can do that is so characteristic of Cary's characters. In this respect she provides a climax to the second group of novels and gives universal force to the formalised aspects of life that are depicted within it.

One other aspect of Tabitha is worth mention: her constant struggle to make her son John and granddaughter Nancy respectable in spite of her own constant readiness to flout convention. She is careful to keep John away from the 'Bankside' crowd and she tries to teach, to bribe even, the child Nancy into saying her prayers. The inconsistency is human enough in itself, but in terms of the development of Cary's vision it foreshadows the need for justification in the world's eyes that underlies the stage three novels that *A Fearful Joy* immediately precedes. Like Gulley, she knows she cannot attain conventional respectability for herself, but unlike him she does not jeer at it on that account. She knows its value and tries to give it to her descendants and so points to the next stage of Cary's development.

Bonser is, for me, a cardboard figure whose repetitive behaviour becomes, in the end, a little tedious. He is a product of Cary's preoccupation with the spellbinder, the man who has the power, by his words and personality to move others to action, but he is too formulaic and there is not enough real life in him to make his ability to arouse Tabitha time after time convincing. He is little more than an animated device.

Nancy, Tabitha's granddaughter, is merely another example of how the permanent in nature will assert itself come what may. She is by Cary's standards, badly raised. She is not taught to say her prayers: Cary was, and looked back approvingly on the experience. She has a concerned but weak father and a mother who is predominantly interested in the world of affairs. Consequently, whilst still a child:

> She has no habit of affection for either of her parents, and she has discovered their helplessness before mere passive resistance and steady lying. . . .
>
> Kit [her mother] cries in despair, 'Really, she won't do a stroke of work unless someone is at her every minute – and I've no time.' John [her father], as he rushes from seminar to committee exclaims, 'It's extraordinary what little interest that child takes in things; she seems completely silly' (*FJ*, pp. 268–9)

She grows into a self-willed and self-indulgent girl. She has a passion for Bonser and becomes, as Cary says, a good-time girl, but she cannot escape her nature. She is a woman, which to Cary meant that she was bound to go through the process of attracting men, having children, rearing them and creating the necessary conditions for this purpose. At the end of the book she goes cheerfully off to New Zealand, delighted that her self-centred husband Joey wants her to accompany him, intent on playing out her role in whatever conditions await her. Though Cary did not intend it, there is pathos in her situation. She will learn nothing, except to adapt to the demands of her environment, and her nature will never change. She is another of life's loyal rank-and-file who will go on and on, doing what she must until death strikes her down. One is reminded of Marie's vision of Bewsher in *An American Visitor* as captain of a rotting galley that would sail on and on to no particular destination, his own corpse being ignominiously disposed of when his time came to die. The underlying vision of life that this image is based on was, I am convinced, Cary's own, and his need to escape from it accounts in large measure for his absolute insistence on the existence of God and his willingness to accept the necessity of the surrender of man's will to that of God as the only satisfactory means of doing so.

5 The Need for Justification

With the completion of *A Fearful Joy*, whose title seems in itself to sum up his own attitude to life, Cary had reached the end of the second stage of the detailed exploration of the vision of life he had postulated in *Aissa Saved*. He had stated his conviction of the necessity of education for life both negatively, in terms of the disaster that lack of it can lead to, and positively, in terms of the benefits of a good upbringing. He had explored the fundamental importance of the permanent in nature and in so doing exposed the limitations of the role of education which, vital though it is, cannot modify nature.

Most of his protagonists, as I have shown, achieve a large degree of subjective success in their search for self-satisfaction at the expense of social failure. Cary's treatment of the problem of human existence up to this point is thus one-sided in that it does not take into account the social element in man's make-up. Self-satisfaction is certainly a basic need, but so is the approval of one's fellows, and it is arguably equally strong. Man not only wants to do what he likes; he wants also to feel justified in doing it. It is not that Cary had totally disregarded it. Aladai, Charley and, most notably, Wilcher all feel the need for it. But he had left it largely out of account in his efforts to convey the ideas he was primarily concerned with in his first and second groups and to this extent had failed to achieve a balanced picture. That he could only proceed step-by-step is undoubtedly a disadvantage to the reader who is not aware of which aspect of Cary's work he is engaged with.

However, he was now ready to bring this aspect of life into account, and, just as the second group did not follow on from *A House of Children* but went back to *Mister Johnson* as a point of departure, so *Prisoner of Grace*, the first of the third group books, does not follow on from *A Fearful Joy*, but takes its departure from the earlier *To Be a Pilgrim*. It is as though Cary, having raised in a substantial way the crux of his next stage, set it aside, perhaps to gestate, completed what he had to say about the aspect he was currently dealing with and then went back, picked it up and gave it his full attention.

In Wilcher, the need for approval arises from his sense of inadequacy. He is socially inept, rather obtuse, and is frequently laughed at for his inability to understand what is perfectly clear to others. There is thus in his efforts to win acceptance a large element of defensiveness that is very reminiscent of Charley with his shaven head. Along with this goes a desire to conceal his true nature, which emerges in incidents like that in which his sister Lucy implies, justly one feels, that he wanted Tolbrook for himself and has secured it at Edward's expense (*TBP*, p. 219). His motives are undoubtedly mixed, so that although it is true to say that he does seek to justify himself, it is not so much because he has a natural need as because he feels the need of a screen to conceal his involuntary motives.

With the third group of protagonists, however, the case is different. They are all convinced that they have acted laudably and are seeking an approval that they believe themselves to have merited. It is in this that the essential difference between them and the second group protagonists lies. Taking Gulley Jimson as the epitome of the latter, we have someone who is thoroughly happy with his own conduct and who knows that it is pointless to expect the world's approbation. But Gulley is a type and in life few, if any, human beings achieve his impregnable self-sufficiency. The third group characters, however, have the human vulnerability that Gulley lacks, and need the reassurance that is superfluous to him, in spite of their conviction of having acted correctly.

It follows from this that it is vital to the consideration of the three novels (i.e. the Second Trilogy) that this group consists of, to accept that the first-person storytellers are all telling the truth as they see it, which raises the question of whether they are reliable or unreliable narrators. The question, of course, is of equal importance to the First Trilogy and the opportunity will therefore be taken to consider the question as a whole. Having said that, however, it must at once be added that because the narrators in the two trilogies are of different kinds, there is not one problem but two.

Fortunately, the First Trilogy can be dealt with quite simply. If it is accepted that the narrators are types of human behaviour rather than representations of human beings, then the question of their being unreliable cannot arise, since they cannot act out of character. Wayne Booth's assertion that Gulley Jimson is an unreliable narrator because his statements cannot be checked,[1] is based upon the mistaken assumption that he is to be regarded as a credible human being. Whilst, therefore, Booth is correct in pointing out that Cary does not provide criteria within the book by which to judge Gulley, to which one may add that this is generally true of Cary's novels, I would maintain that an understanding of the implications of his thinking plus an appreciation of the kind of character he has created in Gulley do enable this omission to be supplied.

The narrators of the Second Trilogy, however, cannot be dealt with in this way. If they are to be regarded as successful representations of human beings, they must be regarded as potentially unreliable. An important factor here is that we know Cary's intention. He makes it plain, for example, in the preface to *Prisoner of Grace*, when discussing the brackets, that this device was expressly designed to make Nina credible:

> Nina telling on her husband, analysing his motives, appeared small and mean, and therefore an unreliable witness . . . she had to be trustworthy in herself or the book became an essay in the cynical   (*PG*, p. 7)

> And when I tried the brackets they did make Nina a credible witness   (*PG*, p. 8)

His concern for his character's credibility must apply equally to the other two volumes. Besides this, as Noble has pointed out,[2] Cary very effectively modifies their diction according to the quality of their utterances. When they are being sincere, they use limpid language that allows the nature of their feelings to be clearly seen. When they are engaged in special pleading or seeking to disguise the truth, their language tends to become elaborate and turbid. The heightened and emotive way in which Nimmo constantly speaks of Nina as a model of womanhood in his refusal to admit her infidelity is a case in point, highlighted by the contrast with the language he uses when speaking of his sister,

Georgina. Nimmo, however, and this is the essential point, is not lying about Nina. He simply refuses to admit the truth to his conscious mind. His need of her is such that he dare not, and if it is objected that such irrational behaviour is confusing to the reader, the answer must be that such behaviour is common enough in life and cannot therefore be out of place in a novel in which, as is once again the case, the characters are credible representations of real human beings, provided that it is signalled to the attentive reader, as in this case it is. Nina's first child by Latter was conceived before marriage. It is not reasonable to suppose that Nimmo could have believed himself to be the father, but perfectly credible that he should refuse to allow himself to recognise Latter's paternity.

The third group narrators, then, are not trying to deceive their audiences. They believe themselves to be telling the truth. The word 'believe' is important, however, for in Cary's books, which are not written in conformity with an extrinsic moral scheme, as in life, the truth is often unknowable. In any case, an important part of the complexity of the Second Trilogy narrators is that they do not understand the extremely limited nature of their freedom, nor that what they are really doing is seeking the satisfaction of their natures. They simply cannot discuss their motives in these terms. Thus Nina explains herself in terms of her realisation of Nimmo's value as a major politician, and seeks justification on the grounds that she has sacrificed herself to his career. Nimmo sees himself in terms of his youthful experience of poverty and religion and seeks to justify himself in terms of his devotion to the cause of the underprivileged. Latter regards himself as a simple English gentleman who knows right from wrong, and claims justification accordingly as a champion of truth and honour. All these motivations are real so far as the characters themselves are concerned. If they were not, as Cary says, the result would be mere cynicism. They are, however, secondary. The search for satisfaction is the prime mover, and the characters must be seen in this light if the books are to be fully understood.

THE SECOND TRILOGY

Nina's duality – what she thinks she is doing on the one hand; what she is really doing on the other – begins to emerge in the very first sentence of her book:

> I am writing this book because I understand that 'revelations' are soon to appear about that great man who was once my husband, attacking his character, and my own. And I am afraid that they will be believed simply because nowadays everyone believes the worst of a famous man. The greater his name, the worse the stories   (*PG*, p. 9)

The key words 'and my own' are easily passed over because the emphasis is on concern for Nimmo, but they are there, and it is apparent that the book is to be an exercise in self-justification as much as the defence of her ex-husband.

A certain ambivalence of attitude towards herself, a divergence between what she claims and what she implies also emerges on the first page, as she continues:

> And first of all, it is not true, as people say, that I was trapped into marriage when I loved someone else. If there was any deceit, it was on my side. But I was barely eighteen at the time and did not know what love was; I don't believe, in fact (as I look back on the creature that I was then), that there was any I to be anything for more than ten minutes at a time.
>
>   But it is true that all these different I's (the one that loved as well as the one that liked reading) were determined to enjoy themselves, and that they were in very close relations with my cousin Jim Latter.

The two statements: 'I . . . did not know what love was' and 'the one that loved' sit ill together, especially when, a little later, she says of Latter's brother, 'I think I was really in love with Bobby (I was only ten, but rather precocious in some feelings) when he went away' (*PG*, p. 11). That Nina really did not know what love was at eighteen is therefore impossible to credit, especially when, much later, we read the following (it is part of a conversation between Latter and Nina on the occasion of his first leave after her marriage to Nimmo):

'I don't think you ever cared for me as I cared for you' [says Latter].

But I would say quite freely, studying the little girl [the young herself] in the miniature, that I had adored Jim. 'It was because it was a real passion that I could not manage it; we were too young to be so badly in love' *(PG*, p. 79)

What is happening on the very first page of the book is that she is being made to reveal the truth about her primary motivation (self-satisfaction) whilst advancing her secondary motivation (the defence of Nimmo) to the fore. For Nina, like the rest of Cary's women since Sara, is primarily a nest builder, and it is this kind of self-satisfaction that she is really seeking.

Her account of what happened over her first child by Latter is presented so as to make herself appear as innocent as possible, but the whole incident is reminiscent of the way Amanda allows herself to be made pregnant by Harry in *The Moonlight* and its import is clear enough. She introduces it thus: 'And when the disaster came to me (if, as I say, looking back on it, you can call it a disaster) and Jim (having for once, poor boy, lost his head with me) . . .' *(PG*, p. 20). But in fact, she has not said anything of the sort, and the feeling that it was not a disaster is reinforced three pages later when she goes on:

So I went to my room and lay down and actually fell asleep. For I was relieved that Aunt knew the position; and as for myself, I was still in that peculiar state that I can only describe as being 'inside' and knowing that it was not nearly so terrible, at least to me, as people 'outside' imagined *(PG*, p. 23)

And the matter is soundly clinched when she finally admits that, '– there was something in Jim's charge that I had "dared" him; we were quarrelling at the time and I had certainly refused to defend myself' *(PG*, p. 25). The initial assertion that Jim has lost his head thus ends in an admission of at least partial responsibility. In Carian terms, Nina is simply satisfying the inevitable demand of her nature. She wanted the child, and is unwittingly admitting to the reader what she cannot admit to herself because she does not know this to have been the case.

Her non-resistance to her aunt's determination to marry her to Nimmo fits this interpretation perfectly. Thus her first reaction,

'I'd rather drown myself', quickly gives way to 'I thought cheerfully that Aunt would arrange something as soon as she got over the shock' (*PG*, p. 23). Similarly, when Nimmo proposes, a note of ambivalence is again struck: 'And before I could say no (or decide what to say) . . .' which quickly gives way to acceptance: 'And when exactly (or how) I accepted Nimmo (but I remember a violent letter from Jim accusing me of "daring" him had a definite effect) I don't know. It simply came to be understood in the next few days' (*PG*, p. 24). What this means is simply that she knew she needed a husband for her nest and a father for her child. Latter was not available because subalterns in his regiment were not allowed to marry and because, in spite of his protestations, 'he had never wanted to marry me. He had preferred the idea of going off to India to play polo' (*PG*, p. 34). Besides, 'Jim (after the disaster) had spoken of marrying me (without making any attempt to do so)' (*PG*, p. 38). Perhaps, too, although she does not say so, she doubted Latter's ability to fulfil the role she required a man to play. He had always treated her cruelly (her own word), whereas Nimmo, in his first proposal, had already made it clear that he was prepared to idolise her.

Amanda, because she lived in a later society than Nina, could dispense with the man, once his biological function was completed, and support her child alone. Nina could not, and because neither man by himself was sufficient for her purpose, was obliged to use both. Latter was virile and sexually attractive, but not domestic. She could use him only to beget the child. Nimmo was apparently sterile (it is noticeable that she likens him to a woman when they are on honeymoon, on p. 26) but could provide an ample and stable home background. Though his attentions were distasteful, he was essential and, instinctively, she knew it.

This is the search for satisfaction with a vengeance – Nina and Shaw's Ann Whitfield are truly two of a kind – and it underlies the whole of her career as a wife. She goes on using Latter as a father and Nimmo as a husband until this is no longer necessary. With her son Tom dead, and her daughter alienated, Nimmo's role is finished. She herself is again pregnant by Latter and, significantly, he is not only much more mature by this time, but also 'by now quite well off' (*PG*, p. 354) and able to support her. So she sends for Latter, not directly, but by going to stay near to his home and tacitly inviting him to seek her out. Her protestations of innocence are not convincing, particularly when, having refused

him admission to her aunt's house because the old lady is in-
flamed against him, she goes on, 'But the result was only that I
had to slip out and see him, and he was so exasperated against me
for my refusing him the house that I could not refuse anything
else' (*PG*, p. 362). The reader is not deceived.

The reason she gives for the divorce is that 'since Chester had
just been defeated again, in the last great disaster of '24, there was
no longer any political reason why I should not be divorced' (*PG*,
p. 360). This, however, is secondary, as the political motivation
always is. After her previous voluntary separation from Nimmo,
she portrays herself as having returned because of her realisation
of his self-sacrifice during the war and her duty to respond. But, in
fact, the conditions were not then right for her to leave him: Tom
was alive and Latter was not only subject to official reprisals but,
having at that point no other income than his pay, was in no
position to provide a home for her. It is this that makes her return
to Nimmo. Her supposed return to grace comes after, when she
feels the need to justify her action. On the first occasion when the
conditions are right and there is no fear of retaliation, she goes.
Her concern for Nimmo is merely a blind to conceal the fact that
she is, though without consciously realising it, using him for her
own ends. Given Cary's view of women, and bearing in mind what
has emerged from the examination of the second group novels, no
other explanation is feasible.

No interpretation of the kind being advanced, however, can be
convincing unless it accounts satisfactorily for the station
waiting-room scene. Cary himself claims in the preface to the
Carfax edition that it was the successful working out of this scene
that satisfied him that the book could be written. His conscious
intention was to show that Nina could not pursue her own happiness at the expense of Nimmo's career, and on the surface this is
what happens. The incident is led up to by direct sequential
narrative from the adultery with Latter in the garden to her
inability to catch the train. That is to say, Nina makes her case as
strongly as she possibly can. But in the description of the after-
math, certain subtle indications are given of other good reasons
for her not leaving Nimmo that must have been present in her
mind at the time, even if not in the forefront. We learn, for
example, that 'Cousin Slapton had refused him [i.e. Jim] the
agency on the grounds that he could not afford to countenance
such a scandal (the whole county was talking about us)' (*PG*,

p. 96). Later, for the information is cleverly scattered and delivered in an incidental and apparently random manner, Aunt
Latter adds: 'I know it's useless to appeal to your better feelings,
but as you pretend to have some affection for Jim you might have
reflected on his very bad position and how important it might be
for him to have a friend [i.e. Nimmo] in Parliament' (*PG*, p. 107).
It is once again clear from these two pieces of information that Jim
was in no position to provide for Nina, her child and her child-to-
be, for, although she cannot know that she is pregnant at first, her
claim, made on p. 101, that she discovered this 'quite unexpec-
tedly' is not convincing. She is revealed throughout the book as an
intelligent woman and after having conceived once already at the
first exchange with Latter, the second pregnancy can hardly be
quite unexpected. She must be stretching the fact here to suit her
purpose. She must also have been aware that Latter's position
would become quite untenable if he outraged society, and she can
hardly have forgotten his desertion of her on the first occasion.
This aspect of the case is made yet stronger by the way in which,
by her own account, his attitude changed as soon as he had
possessed her:

> now Jim had forgotten himself so passionately and made sure of
> me, as he said, he was the old Jim again; he had stopped being
> respectful to me or polite about Chester. But in my mood at the
> moment he could, as I said, have done anything he liked to
> me   (*PG*, p. 86)

It is hard to avoid concluding that she must have been influenced
by these considerations at the time of the waiting-room incident
and did not merely become aware of them later as her narrative
suggests.

Love apart, she had a great deal to lose by leaving Nimmo at
this point. The material aspect of her potential loss is underlined
by her reaction to life at Johnson's, 'which was the most expensive
hotel in Britain', to which Nimmo cleverly insists on sending her
to recover. The relevant passage, which is too long to quote,
begins on p. 101 with the words 'And from this time . . .' and ends
on p. 103 with the words '. . . I'm not going to fight about trifles'.

The first point to be made is that Nina needs, and responds to
luxury, as Nimmo realises. It is not very hard to imagine a woman
who can admit to responding to it in the way Nina does, holding

back from the life that a discredited, penniless and uncertain-tempered Latter could have offered. She claims to have been in misery, but she does not fail to notice how becoming to her its flattering effect on her appearance is when she looks in the mirrors, and it takes her only a single week to start taking an interest in politics and world affairs, though 'in a dignified sad way' of course. That makes all the difference! Irony is seen again in the considerate absence of protest at the expensive frock Nimmo buys for her in Bond Street. This is a rather naïve attempt to dissemble, and nothing more. If a clincher is needed, it occurs in the comparison she makes between Nimmo and Latter as spenders. Nimmo is a royal spender who makes sure that he always has money at his disposal; Latter is a scatterer (the word is clearly used pejoratively in the context) who, by implication here, and in fact too as it turns out later, has no control over it. Latter is clearly being shown at a disadvantage.

The final clue to Nina to be found in this episode occurs very appropriately at the end of it, when she leaves the hotel: 'the more I thought of it, the more I realized how important it was for me (in the selfish sense) that Chester should have a big success. I was extremely anxious to help him' (*PG*, p. 108). This is because: 'I was able to see for the first time the important *fact* that if Chester lost the election I might have to blame myself for it' (*PG*, p. 107). But this realisation comes after the waiting-room scene. The exact time is not specified but it is certainly rather more than a week, since Nina does not begin to read the newspapers again until 'after a week' and this happens some days, perhaps a week or two, after that – in other words, after she has had plenty of time to enjoy the luxury that Nimmo has provided and reflect at leisure upon the consequences of leaving him for Latter. The reasonable assumption is that her realisation is in fact a rationalisation, designed to cloak with respectability and even honour a decision made for other reasons.

This matches well her account of the waiting-room incident, for when that is examined again it is noticeable that, although writing many years (over a quarter of a century) after the event, she provides no reason for not catching the train:

> When I reached the door (of the waiting-room) my feet stopped and turned me aside. I simply could not go out, and neither could I make up my mind to stay. I went a step to one side, and

then came back to the door, but absolutely stuck there. I seemed to have no will to do anything, or rather I had two wills which were fighting inside me and tearing me apart. I can never forget the agony of that time, which must actually have lasted three or four minutes before the train went out. And really I think it was a kind of relief to me when at last it did so, for it made a decision for me *(PG*, pp. 95–6)

There is little sign of Nimmo's grace here. The election has not yet entered her mind. She is faced with a straightforward choice between the man she loves and the man who can provide the nest she needs, and she chooses the provider, for although she claims that the train made the decision for her, this is clearly specious. There was only one 'decision' it could make. The plea that she stayed because Nimmo needed her can thus once more be seen to lack conviction. She stayed because she needed him, and the real reason why it was important to her that Nimmo should have a big success can be seen in this. Hence her anxiety to help him.

Further evidence that Nimmo is her real choice at this point comes in the next chapter. The incident with Mr Mockley, an old family friend but a political opponent, confirms the suggestion that Nina behaves instinctively rather than rationally that is implicit in the statement that her feet stopped and turned her aside in the waiting-room: 'When he came smiling to shake hands (I meant to be polite at least) my hand simply jumped away from his and then my eyes looked through him and my legs (trembling with shame as well as political indignation) walked past him' *(PG*, p. 109). This is not the action of a woman who makes her decisions in a reasoned manner, on grounds of conscience and at the expense of her nature; and the placing of the two instances so close together seems to nullify any suggestion that they are without significance. In any case, she goes on:

And in the same way when Jim wrote furious letters, suggesting that I was being 'kept for him', and threatening to come and 'have it out' with Chester, I was quite horrified by such a suggestion. I answered by return begging him to be patient (pointing out that, on account of my condition alone, I was absolutely his – it was only a question of time before I came to him for good), with long explanations of the critical position at

Tarbiton, and how terribly important it was for both our sakes
that Chester should win   (*PG*, p. 109)

One notices first the words, 'And in the same way': this is a third
instance of the same, instinctive, kind of behaviour. Next, one
realises that the words in brackets (the words that according to
Cary make Nina a reliable witness) are a classic instance of
'putting off'. Finally, one asks why it was important for Latter that
Chester should win. Surely the reverse was the case: his only
chance was that Nimmo's career should fail to materialise.

This and the whole tone of the chapter raise the question of
whether Nina, far from being a reluctant heroine, is not heart and
soul in the election alongside Nimmo. She has already said: 'I was
extremely anxious to help him – to be driven through the streets in
a landau, with Tommy on my knee, and to address letters, to
canvass the back lanes and Slapton tenants, and to go to chapel
tea-parties' (*PG*, p. 108). At first sight, everything except the main
clause in this sentence has an ironic flavour, but the true meaning
only emerges when the unspoken rider, 'Unpleasant though all
these things are in themselves', is added. For of Latter she says,
'What is he worrying about?' and 'Doesn't he realize what an
election means?'; of Nimmo, 'He showed . . . all his courage and
good humour, his marvellous resourcefulness', and, indirectly, of
herself, 'The women, especially, adored him and were quite
comically jealous of me as his wife' (*PG*, p. 109). It is hard not to
believe that she relished this situation, that Nimmo and the
election were everything and Latter, at this point, nothing.

By the end of the election she and Nimmo have achieved a new
rapport: 'we were both staggering with weariness and drunk with
triumph. But we were still talking both at once about that extraordinary last day (we had so much to tell each other)' (*PG*,
p. 111), and it is only when he wants to follow her into her
bedroom to assume Latter's role as lover that the mood vanishes.
And this is quite consistent with the argument being advanced:
taking everything into account, she needs Nimmo more than
Latter, but that need not prevent her from preferring Latter as a
lover. As for the excitement of the political life being part of what
she wants from Nimmo, this would also account for the fact that
she does not leave him until his political career has finally ended.
On the evidence of this episode, it is certainly feasible that she is as
much concerned with her own need as his, and if the reading of

Cary's vision of life that is being advanced is accurate, then there can be no difficulty in accepting that she is more concerned with it.

For if what Cary claims for her in the title of the book is true, she is a mere aberration, another of those characters in his work whose essential vitality has failed and who, instead of seeking to create their own lives, merely allow themselves to be used. But nowhere else does Cary make such a character the subject of a major study, and in spite of his declared intention, Nina is not an exception. It is true that in his preface he states that 'The book was called *Prisoner of Grace* because Nina was held to her husband by the sense that he was on the whole a good man' (*PG*, p. 6), and there can be no denying that he saw Nimmo as the creator and Nina as his tool, but he quite overlooked the fact that Nina, in terms of his own assertions about the permanent in nature, was bound to have purposes of her own and that in her pursuit of them she would only submit to being Nimmo's tool for as long as she could make him hers. In fact, the provision by Cary of an explanation that does not fit his own rules is a clear indication that, whereas the thinker in him did not fully appreciate the implications of his ideas, the artist, operating from a deeper level of consciousness, both understood them perfectly and acted upon them. The search for satisfaction is unlikely to be the whole truth about human motivation, but it is self-evidently both a major motivating force and a convincing concept, giving point to human vitality and activity. It does not rule out the possibility of what is generally called disinterested action, such as he claims for Nina, but it does, by making it either a means to or a form of satisfaction in its own right, change the accepted meaning of that word. No sane person, not even the suicider, deliberately does himself harm: pain, when it is voluntarily borne, is always accepted because it is somehow conducive to satisfaction, of which, to the Cary woman, the need to make a home and raise children is the prime source.

So it is with Nina. Throughout her life she does nothing but what is likely to give herself the greatest possible satisfaction. She cannot have everything she would like, of course, and sometimes she is obliged to accept the smallest evil rather than obtain the greatest pleasure, but she is not a victim, nor is she anybody's prisoner. The point is made explicitly in terms of her married relationship to Latter:

once he even trusted me with the dangerous idea that I had
changed for the better, that I seemed to have learnt at last that
even a pretty girl can't have it all her own way.

I did not dare to tell him that if this was true he owed a great
deal of the new woman to Chester's skilful discipline　(*PG*,
p. 365)

She has learnt, that is, how to appear to be giving way, whilst
really making the most effective compromise, the one that gives
the greatest possible satisfaction, and making it as a matter of
policy, not, as in her earlier life, as a matter of necessity after
running her head needlessly against brick walls, as in the
waiting-room incident. Her success is to be measured by her
comment, occurring a page earlier in the same passage of reflection, that 'so far from being Jim's slave, I belonged to myself more
intensely than ever in my life before'. She has learnt how to live,
and is at this point triumphant. Having had everything that she
could obtain from Nimmo, she is now obtaining the remainder of
what she wants from Latter. She is as successful as it is possible for
anyone to be in Cary's world and is the culmination of all that he
has been working towards. She overcomes the problems of youth
and ignorance that destroyed the early protagonists; she is a
credible representation of a human being and not a type-
character as are the protagonists of the middle period. She is
complex and coherent, and she provides a convincing example of
how, according to Cary the artist, life has to be lived.

Nina's book is thus not to be read at its face value, that is to say
at Cary the theorist's valuation of it. It is to be seen as the attempt
of an intelligent woman to justify herself in terms of the ethos of a
society that expects its members to behave selflessly. But it is an
unconscious attempt. Nina herself believes in that ethic, as Cary
did. She really does think that she has sacrificed herself to
Nimmo's career, and refused to indulge herself at his expense, as
Cary did. She really does see herself as a helpless pawn in
Nimmo's hands, as Cary did. And it is the fact that none of these
things is true that gives the book its fundamental value, for what
emerges is Cary's unrealised but unshakable belief that life is not
like that at all. We do what we must, and justify it as best we can,
and the answer to the question of whether or not we have any
freedom beyond a limited choice of means remains a very doubtful
one indeed; for if Nina is, after all, a prisoner, then it is to her own

nature, not to Nimmo, that she is in thrall. Not once does she ever act in opposition to its dictates. Not once does she ever show any sign of having the power to do so. The morality which Cary claims for her is an illusion.

It remains now to account for Nina's death. She claims that she tolerates Nimmo's sexual assaults when she is helping him with his memoirs because

> now, more than ever, at the end of his life, I was in his power. . . . I knew that he held me still with a thousand ties that I should never break – ties from a marriage of nearly thirty years that was all the more 'part of me' because I had suffered in it   (*PG*, p. 400)

But since at the same time she claims to be more in love with Latter than ever before, this too fails to convince. The precise nature of the ties is not specified. The idea that she cannot dissociate herself from a relationship because it had caused her to suffer against her will is odd: one would expect the opposite to be the case. One is left wondering just how real her protests are.

Though she is careful (in accordance with the social ethics of sex of the time) always to portray herself as having sexual relations only at the behest of either Latter or Nimmo, one is left with the definite impression that she herself is quite highly sexually motivated. The amount and type of reference she makes to it go beyond what the context warrants, especially if one considers the book as reflecting her writing in the context of the middle 1920s rather than Cary writing in that of the early 1950s. However, at neither date had the vogue for public explicitness about sex reached its present pitch. If this is not to be attributed to faulty writing by Cary, and he is surely too good a writer for that and too concerned to give the authentic feel of the historic background, then Nina's preoccupation with sex must be regarded as indicating that the sexual aspect of her nature is well developed. More, it would seem that she has some public reputation of this kind. When she and Nimmo retire to bed at the end of the election that follows the waiting-room scene and results in Nimmo becoming a Member of Parliament, she precedes her account of what happened with these words: 'Now I have to explain what happened on this occasion because of this other charge that "I corrupted" my poor husband, not only in soul but body' (*PG*, p. 113). What the charge is based on and how it arose are not revealed. What matters is that she has a reputation for sexual corruptness and both feels the need to defend herself and in so doing to reveal her practice. Just for a moment the Wife of Bath again seems to cast her shadow.

What happens at this point, of course, is that she initiates Nimmo into the Indian technique that she has learnt from Latter. Her claim is that she does it only to satisfy Nimmo and be rid of him. This may be so, but it may equally be the case that she was not averse to repeating the experience for its own sake. At least, she never shows any aversion to sex and is always ready to commit adultery with Latter whenever he wishes, as well as cope with the demands of Nimmo, whose own sexual energies and needs are shown to be considerable. Evidence for this is to be found, for example, in the words of the doctor, Sir Connell T., who comes to see her when she goes to stay at Buckfield during the Great War, and tells her that if she does not continue to satisfy Nimmo, he will hold her responsible if Nimmo's health gives way (*PG*, p. 299).

More definite evidence of her positive enjoyment of sex is to be found in her relation of the incident in which Nimmo makes love to her in a horse-drawn cab. It occurs early in the marriage, when he was first elected a county councillor, but is not related until the time of his first assault upon her, when he alludes to it indirectly to remind her of the experiences they have shared, something he would surely not do if he thought it would produce an adverse reaction. He is too clever a politician for that. Her description of the incident is both equivocal and suggestive. She begins by saying that 'the whole affair . . . was very muddled and desperate, and in fact, rather a failure', but after revealing that 'both of us were anxious not to spoil it for the other' and referring to the moment when 'we were both at our most exalted moment' (an indication in itself that she was enjoying the experience), she says that 'afterwards, when we were at peace in bed, we fell asleep in each other's arms, still feeling that at last we had been admitted into wonderful secrets and mysteries', and ends with the statement that 'in the morning the wonders had vanished' (*PG*, pp. 395–6). A strange failure! The initial attempt to dissemble is destroyed by the final admission of her intense enjoyment of the experience, which she still feels strongly after an interval of perhaps a quarter of a century.

It is evident that Nina herself has both an ample sexual appetite and the ability to enjoy whatever comes her way, and that this fact must at least cast doubt on her statement that she was unable to dismiss Nimmo merely because she was in his power. The doubt is heightened when her account of the first assault is examined, for it then appears that what frightened and angered her was not the fact of the assault but the manner of it. There had always been a 'spiritual' element in Nimmo's attentions, 'but now he attacked me in quite a different way, as I suppose unfortunate girls are attacked in trains or on lonely commons' (*PG*, p. 385). The fact that she returns to Palm Cottage the very next day when her daughter comes to fetch her would seem to indicate that she rapidly acclimatises even to this. Few women, surely, will submit to being sexually assaulted either for old times' sake or as a matter of duty, especially if, as Nina claims herself to be, she is in love with a man of a very jealous and uncertain temperament. Can it be that she finds these experiences as stimulating as does Nimmo himself? Certainly, she very quickly finds excuses for him by comparing his behaviour with that of the aged Goethe and Tolstoy, the implication that Nimmo is cast in their mould making it all the more 'right' for her to co-operate: '(and now I did everything possible to give the man what he wanted, simply to get it over)' (*PG*, p. 388) is her claim, but it does not ring true.

Thus, whilst it is not possible to assert categorically that Nina welcomed Nimmo's assaults, it is difficult not to be very sceptical about the reason she gives for tolerating them. Apart from what has been said so far, it is noticeable also that the final situation between herself, Latter and Nimmo is a simple reversal of the original one, the men having changed places. It is arguable, therefore, that she still needs them both, husband and lover, and that she dies, still seeking the satisfaction her nature demands, because, unlike Nimmo, Latter cannot, when he is in ostensible possession of the female, tolerate the presence of the other male. As a woman who sacrifices first her happiness and finally her life to the career of a man she does not love, Nina is not credible: she lacks the moral stature. But as a woman who goes through life obeying the dictates of her nature and who dies because she is powerless to change it, she is. Seen in this light, she even acquires tragic stature.

Nimmo, in *Except the Lord*, presents himself as a crusader, motivated by early experience of poverty and injustice and sustained by his political idealism. Nina represents him as a great man who, if he needed to use other people in the pursuance of his aims, was justified in so doing. Latter represents him as a self-seeking crook. Cary himself intends him as 'an adventurer not only for his own career but for a cause he thought good' (*PG*, p. 7), and asserted, in the preface to *Prisoner of Grace*, that although Nimmo had been called a crook, he was not meant to be one. He agreed, however, that he was not a completely admirable character.

It is easy now to agree with Cary, if only because, during the thirty or so years since the book was published, the true nature of the politician has become more widely known as a result of the activities of the media. Cary's picture of the politician as a man who, whilst he may be sincere, is not more scrupulous than any other about promoting his own welfare is clearly accurate.

Nimmo is a typical Cary character in so far as, like all of them except Syson, he runs on fixed lines, but in one important way he forms a contrast with Nina. In her case, the main emphasis is on the inherent factor: in his it is, as in the earlier case of Aladai, on the environmental; that is to say, Cary takes up once again his theme of education. In the typescript that has already been referred to on p. 60, beginning 'Education is teaching . . .', having stressed the importance of the pre-school years and quoted a master as saying that schools can do no more than salvage, Cary goes on:

> I think this is true even of those young genii who climb right out of their environment and out of illiterate homes to become great scholars and statesmen. They are still deeply affected by their earliest lessons. Of course those lessons are largely moral – illiterate parents can still give their children a sound moral character.

Except that his parents were literate, this fits Nimmo. Here he is talking about his early religious experience with his mother:

> When I knelt in her lap and whispered my first prayers into her breast, I cannot tell what ideas that bedtime ceremony stirred in my infant mind. But was I wrong to feel that I knelt in a holy place and communicated with a spirit which was then in all its gentle and modest service truly one with the most High?

Confused ideas they were in a small child, and more feelings
than ideas. But all the deeper, all the more powerful to guard
me after that lap and that breast were dust   (*EL*, p. 11)

This is not to say, of course, that Nimmo is exclusively the
product of education, even in the wide sense in which Cary uses
that word. He too has his fixed nature, which in his case is a
combination of that of the leader and the spellbinder, two types
which Cary acknowledged himself to be concerned with and
which recur throughout his work. Coker (*The African Witch*) and
Bonser (*A Fearful Joy*) come readily to mind as spellbinders in his
earlier books, and Bewsher (*An American Visitor*), Cock Jarvis (*Cock
Jarvis*) and Charley (*Charley Is My Darling*) as leaders. Nimmo is
particularly interesting in that in his case fixed nature is seen
being reinforced by education. To distract his attention when the
family's farm is being sold up, his mother begins to tell him a
story: ' "Once upon a time there was a little boy called, What do
you think?" I answered, with a deep sense of penetration and
cunning, my own name. My mother often told us stories in which
we were the heroes and I especially revelled in them' (*EL*, p. 11).
The idea of himself as central character, common enough in
children, strikes a stronger chord in Nimmo than in his brother
and sister because he alone of them is the born leader and needs to
rehearse his future role. Like Molière, he seizes on the material he
needs wherever he happens to find it and uses it for his own
purposes. Its importance to him is underlined by the fact that,
although writing some seventy years later, he remembers and
inserts it. The information is not otherwise either significant or
necessary to his story.

A parallel experience brings into his consciousness his latent
power as a spellbinder. He and his sister, Georgina, see a performance of *Maria Marten*. She is glad to have seen Corder hanged as
punishment for his crimes but

> I was still beneath a different spell – a feeling, an illumination
> that I could not describe, preoccupied my mind. . . . I felt the
> evil of that power [i.e. that of the theatre] and dreaded it. But I
> also understood a power that I had seen exercised by my father
> also – though in a lesser degree – that of the orator.
>
>   For me the actor had a fearful, an astonishing power – one
> that entranced my boy's soul not only by its imposing solitary

glory, but perhaps even more profoundly by its defiance. And this was a power that could be achieved by anyone with the will and a voice, anyone capable of learning this art of stringing words together in poetic form, and striking the right attitudes. For Georgina he was a rich and selfish squire's son, a cruel brute, as the Martens represented the deprived and suffering poor   (*EL*, pp. 98–9)

The existence of fixed nature in the two children is emphasised by the complete disparity of their responses. The spellbinder responds in Nimmo; the demander of justice in his sister. The leader, too, responds actively in Nimmo, for he sees the use he can make of the spellbinder's powers:

> There was planted in this rough dirty boy who now spoke habitually, as in spite against his lot, the broadest and crudest dialect, a vision of glory, of power, by means of the spoken word.
>
> I say that power was a fantasy to me – I had yet no idea of achievement. But the idea can exist without the hope . . .
>
> My first audience was Mrs. Coyte's sheep, or simply the rocks and gorse on some hillside   (*EL*, p. 111)

The middle paragraph of this quotation is again a clear indication of the working of fixed nature.

In general, however, it is not possible to make as strong a case for Nimmo's being at the mercy of his nature as it is in the case of Nina, and for these reasons. She, though intelligent, is an unsophisticated user of words, and constantly says more than she realises. Nimmo, on the other hand, is a master of the art of giving words the meaning he wants them to convey. He is convinced that he has acted selflessly throughout his career in response to life as he has experienced it and that his actions have been freely determined by himself, and he constructs his case accordingly, leaving few loopholes. Cary's skill as a writer, his ability to assume the role he is creating, is thus well reflected in both characters. Nimmo, too, has been able to choose his ground to much greater advantage than Nina. She was acting defensively, seeking largely to justify herself in the light of events that are public knowledge against a public attack that she cannot prevent. Nimmo, on the other hand, has seized the initiative and is attempting to get his blow in first. His boyhood was obscure and took place among simple people, most of whom must be dead at the time of writing. He is simply not open to scrutiny in the same way that Nina is.

What we see in Nimmo, in fact, is a taking up of the threads that were dropped with the completion of *A House of Children*. Nimmo is the antithesis, the sublimation even, of all the first group worldly failures. Their attempts to create their own worlds were thwarted by their lack of education: his are made successful by the possession of it. Nimmo himself emphasises the point:

> A child brutalized before puberty is a child lost – for all the forces of his growing pour into that rage of appetites. How much I owed in those dark days to the custom of my daily prayer, to the knowledge of my father's goodness, to the care of my sister? I did not, indeed, realize what these things meant to me, I would mutter the few words of supplication half asleep; my father's reading . . . passed my understanding . . . but my memory, despite myself, was full of songs   (*EL*, p. 110)

The contrast with Charley (*Charley Is My Darling*) and the comparison with Evelyn (*A House of Children*) are too apparent to need detailing. The stress on education throws the over-riding importance of fixed nature somewhat into the background, but it does not destroy it. The education enables the fixed nature to operate successfully. Together with the historical environment (Cary's point in *The Moonlight*) it provides both the specific ends and the expertise necessary for their achievement, even though it does not modify nature. Given other environmental experience, Nimmo might not have been a politician, nor a Christian, nor even a success, but he would have been a spellbinder and a leader, even though he had destroyed himself in the process of trying to give effect to his nature, as all his first group forerunners, except Evelyn, did; and he would have been, and is, no more free than Gulley and the other second group protagonists to be anything else.

In the event, Nimmo is public-spirited as well as self-seeking. In so far as he progressively abandons his ideals – trades unionism, Marxism, land nationalisation – and becomes a capitalist who is clearly prepared, in spite of Nina's defence of him (*PG*, p. 214), to indulge in insider share dealing in the Contract Case, he is a man of low integrity who can be seen at every move to be motivated by the desire for power and wealth. Sometimes, as when he abandons Marxism and trades unionism together during the Lilmouth strike, he is cutting his losses. In that instance, having lost his value to Pring, he merely anticipates dismissal and quits an unfruitful course of action. At other times, as when he gives up his pacifism for a seat in the Cabinet, he is in direct pursuit of power, the self-satisfaction that by nature he cannot deliberately forgo. The kind of action that he deplores in others, for example, the attacks on Gadd's carters and the proposed attack on Brodribb in *Except the Lord*, he perpetuates himself when he allows Maufe and Bell to be sacrificed in *Not Honour More*. It is easy to see why he has been described as a crook.

Yet at the same time, his desire to benefit his fellow-citizens is real. At the outset at least, he is genuinely moved by the plight of the poor and, once he is launched into politics, he can only make his way by instigating and supporting beneficial policies. Whatever his real motives, and I can see no grounds for regarding him as a complete cynic, he has a vested interest in promoting the public weal. But to do this he, like any politician, must achieve power, must do whatever is necessary to achieve it, and must deceive and manipulate in order to exercise it. In 'Personal and Political Morality', Cary says:

> It has been said that government is making people do what they don't like, since they will cheerfully follow their own inclinations without any instruction; and that in the final resort there are only two ways of making them act against their own inclinations. To shoot the disobedient or to wangle them. If you include under shooting every kind of coercion; if you include under wangling every kind of persuasion, such as an appeal to conscience, to patriotic or family feeling, to self-respect or self-interest, then this is true. And it is the last method which is the only one open to the government of a free democracy. They are not allowed to shoot.[3]

Nimmo is thus of necessity a wangler, something that Latter is incapable of understanding. A statesman must be accounted honest if he means well and tries to do well: the ends justify the means in Cary's world. Nimmo fulfils these criteria. As a type of the practical politician he rings true.

He is also a character of considerable complexity: self-deceived and rather pathetic where Nina is concerned, yet at the same time shrewd in his determination to hold on to a valuable political asset; self-seeking where money and prestige are concerned; an unscrupulous politician when power is at stake; and yet, with it all, a true statesman. He is capable, too, of genuine admiration for natures different from his own, in particular that of his sister Georgina, who fulfils her role as a Cary woman to perfection, refusing an advantageous marriage and hastening, if not actually causing, her own death by her unwillingness to abandon the nest she has taken over from her mother. I find him utterly convincing.

Latter (*Not Honour More*) is a development of the first group protagonists, and as such forms a convenient and effective yard-stick against which to measure the distance that Cary has moved in the creation of Nina and Nimmo. Latter, as he is made to reveal himself in his book, has not moved from the child's love of fixed, simple, readily approvable values and relationships. He is men-tally a child still, who does not understand the adult world and fails to see why he cannot have his own way all the time. Whatever does not conform to his own idea of things is false, rotten and crooked. All that is wanted to put things right is a few honest men who are not out for themselves and will do what is clearly their duty. His vision of life is egocentric, grossly over-simple and quite unrealistic.

What really sets the seal on Latter's immaturity is the duality of his standards. For all his talk of honour, and it is, of course, by posing as a man of honour that he seeks to justify himself, he never hesitates to commit adultery with another man's wife, and never sees any wrong in it. In fact he regards it in a curiously inverted way as establishing his right to her. 'That's all right then. Now you belong to me, and you can never have anything to do with that poop stick again – not if you have a grain of honourable feeling in you' (*PG*, p. 86), he says after committing adultery with Nina in the garden when on his first leave. This is schoolboy logic, and he uses it continually. For example, his gambling debts must be paid before those to his tradesmen, because they are debts of honour; but all this means is that he wants them paid first so that he can become socially acceptable again. Paying the tradesmen offers no such advantage. Honour thus equals selfishness. His 'honour' is also revealed as a sham when, having made Nina pregnant the first time he goes off to India to play polo and leaves her to be married off to Nimmo.

Other characteristics of immaturity abound. When he is sent to Africa as a condition of being saved from his creditors, he sees himself as a victim. He makes large claims on behalf of Sergeant Varney in order to bask in his reflected glory and boost his own standing: 'One of the best, one of the finest, truest chaps in the world. And he's my Sergeant' (*NHM*, p. 77). He constantly uses schoolboy slang. He is invariably rude to people he does not agree with, calling Bootham 'fat boy', for example. He condemns people for the ideas he supposes them to hold without bothering to check his facts, as is illustrated by his conversation with Sally about Brightman: '[Sally] said at once, "I mean calling Major Brightman a Fascist as if that was enough to prove he wasn't worth anything. And you admit you've never listened to him or read anything by him." I said that was true but I thought I had a pretty good idea of his line' (*NHM*, p. 143). When words, often in the form of insults, fail him, he regularly resorts to violence, and eventually gives himself the power of life and death over those whose conduct does not accord with his own ideas. He is a thoroughly selfish, thoroughly spoilt child, incapable of any form of self-questioning and therefore of self-judgement and change.

Latter is thus an outstanding example of untutored fixed nature seeking self-satisfaction with terrifying energy and determination. He was encouraged in this by Aunt Latter during his boyhood:

> Now, Nina, you're not to be a nuisance to Jimmy these holidays. Remember he has no proper home, poor boy, and we must make this a home for him. If he wants to do things, do them willingly. Don't forget that Jimmy is very proud. He does not like to be under obligations – especially to little girls　(*PG*, p. 10)

There is also some evidence that his disposition was inborn. Speaking of his father, Nina says: 'But Jim always hated him and had been such a trouble to him that everyone was glad when Aunt Latter arranged to take him for the holidays' (*PG*, p. 11). No reason is given for this hatred and the father is not presented unsympathetically. It would seem to be innate.

Immaturity and ignorance are thus very much to the fore once again in the case of Latter, but, in spite of that, he is not a simple repeat of a first group protagonist, in spite of the resemblance he bears to Bewsher in being, as a colonial district officer, a pagan man whose African subjects turn against him. In their cases, it will be remembered, death or, in Charley's case, incarceration, put so quick an end to their careers that the question of whether they could have overcome their disabilities remained open. But at the end of his life Latter is fifty (he refers to Nina as being forty-six and she says that he is four years her senior) and, unlike any of his first group predecessors, he has been before us for much of that time. He has had every opportunity, and nothing has happened.

The failure of education is thus complete in Latter, not because it lacks the power to bring about the desired change, but because Latter was not subjected to it at an early enough age. Cary's insistence upon the importance of the early years will be remembered, strongly expressed as it is both in 'Education is teaching . . .' and in Nimmo's belief that the brutalisation of the pre-adolescent was permanent. Just as Nimmo is the antithesis of the first group failures, so Latter is the antithesis of Nimmo, for whereas Nimmo was saved by his early contact with religion from the adverse effect of his poverty-stricken environment, Latter, in spite of his much more privileged background, suffers badly as an adult from early lack of guidance and loving care. He is raw nature. He contrasts also, of course, with the young Evelyn, who, coming from the same stratum of society, did receive the appropriate upbringing, just as Nimmo contrasts in his turn with the young Charley, who came from the same stratum as Nimmo and did not.

Their relationships confirm what has often been noted about Cary, that he uses and re-uses his basic material. They also indicate that merely to make this observation and to regard some characters as forerunners of others is not enough. The relationships between characters in the different books are often illuminating when seen in the total context of Cary's work, which must be seen as a whole to be fully appreciated.

Apart from being the definitive version of the first group characters, however, Latter also has strong links with the second group protagonists, for although he is presented as a credible human being and not as the type of a single mode of behaviour, as, for example, Gulley Jimson is, he comes over not so much as a man with certain characteristics as the embodiment of those characteristics in a man. He never acts so as to surprise the reader, even for an instant, and, perhaps because he is totally lacking in guile, he leaves behind no feeling that he is capable of doing so, no feeling of hidden depth. He is a concentration and a refinement of what he portrays, in a way that Nina and Nimmo are not, and yet he exists in their world and interacts successfully with them. He may therefore be said to span the three groups and to sum up, in so far as any one character can, the sombre aspect of the view of the human lot that Cary's work embodies.

This view of Latter is, I think, reinforced by his end. In taking upon himself the powers of judgement and of life and death, he in effect exalts himself into a god and so makes a desperate attempt to achieve Cary's ultimate solution to man's predicament, identity with the will of God. He fails, partly because his action is tantamount to suicide and is thus indicative of despair, and partly because, being both immature and arrogant, he assumes a role that he cannot sustain. What is interesting is that totally inadequate and misguided though he is, he nevertheless has some inkling that man alone cannot resolve his own dilemma and in this respect his action matches Nimmo's return to religion at the end of his life. With all his faults, he tries.

In spite of their relationships with earlier characters, however, both Latter and Nimmo exhibit the characteristic third group need for justification. Their cases are much more straightforward than that of Nina because the actions they seek to justify have been much more public, in Nimmo's case especially, and they do not feel the need to reveal such intimate details of their private lives as she does. They paint their pictures in broader strokes and bolder colours. Yet they all have one thing in common that both links them, thus strengthening the artistic unity of the trilogy, and emphasises the development in Cary's work since the creation of Wilcher, their progenitor. All three make their bids for justification under virtual sentence of death. Nina cannot know that she will be murdered, but the last sentence of her book clearly indicates her awareness of its likelihood: 'Jim can only shoot me dead'. Nimmo is old, exhausted from a career of furious activity, has a weak heart, and is still driving himself. Latter is facing the gallows. They are all therefore at least as much, arguably more, concerned with posthumous reputation as current. When this is compared with Wilcher's attitude when he realises that death is imminent, the difference is striking. He gives up both the world and the good opinion of the world that he has striven for so long, and finds both consolation and satisfaction in the acknowledgement of his true nature. They, because they are not aware of their true natures, nor what motivates them, strive the harder to establish the images of themselves that they have created, have had to create, to justify the response to the demands of their own natures that they could not help making. This is the essential Carian paradox, and, paradoxically, it depends not upon the fact that man is free, as Cary the inadequate theorist thought, but upon the fact that he is held captive by the demands of his nature, and is forced to seek refuge in what is little more than the illusion of freedom.

The Second Trilogy thus needs to be read at two levels. First, there is the ostensible level, on which the explanations that the characters give of their own conduct are not merely believed by them to be true but, at this level, are so. Michael J. C. Echeruo, in his *Joyce Cary and the Dimensions of Order*, has given an admirable discussion of this aspect of the novels, revealing Nina and Nimmo in particular as Cary intended them to be seen, for there can be no doubt that their own views of themselves are Cary's and that they are justified from their own points of view. But it is also necessary to be aware of the permanent and inescapable state of affairs that, in Cary's world and perhaps – who knows? – in the real world too, underlies all human conduct. Nina, Nimmo and Latter are mistaken about their own motives. They are convinced that they are moral beings capable of disinterested action, whereas in reality they are amoral, acting only in response to the demands of their natures and seeking only to gratify themselves, a goal which is, as Cary saw quite clearly, unattainable. Their disinterestedness is merely a cloak which they wear in order to justify themselves in the eyes of the world whilst under its cover they pursue their own ends. But of course this does not prevent them from having done what they claim. Nina has been of great value to Nimmo and his tributes to her are, her adultery apart, justified. Nimmo has been a major politician and has made a genuine contribution to the development of society. Nina's valuation of him is valid. At the same time, both have dissimulated and are worthy of Latter's criticism. Latter does advocate and try to put into effect an open and honourable mode of public conduct, and Nimmo's appreciation of his sense of honour (*NHM*, p. 2) is valid also. In other words, the world's work gets done, and done as well as it can be done in a world in which ideals are always frustrated and injustice is endemic, but for the wrong reasons: it is not an end in itself but a by-product of the pursuit of self-satisfaction, the nature and general direction of change being determined by the approximate coincidence of need in the majority.

For the individual there is no final satisfaction. Nina has her throat cut, Nimmo is hounded to death in a WC and Latter, it must be assumed, will be hanged. Nina and Nimmo die because they will not do what Latter wants and he dies because he is immature enough to believe that he has the right to put to death people who are not prepared to subordinate their needs to his. Nina achieves true though limited insight into the nature of things when she realises that the simple and restful life she was looking forward to on leaving Nimmo for Latter is not only unforthcoming but that life as a result 'is even more difficult and complicated than ever' (*PG*, p. 301) and there is irony in her remark that 'To turn Chester out would be to commit a mean crime against something bigger than love' (*PG*, p. 301). She means that she would be neglecting her obligation to Nimmo's grace, but the deeper meaning is that she would be denying her own need for self-satisfaction, denying the very principle on which life is founded and so denying life itself. Her real duty is to do what she must and take the consequences, as indeed she does.

Nimmo, too, moves towards the truth. His return to religion foreshadows Cary's own conclusion, to be fully explored in his final book *The Captive and the Free*, that only an unconditional surrender to God can give man the total satisfaction he seeks. On the ostensible level, his attempt to bring about a just society by means of political activity having failed, he ceases to put his faith in man and transfers it back to God. In terms of the search for satisfaction, the spellbinder and leader in him, having been denied further outlet via politics, turns back to preaching. The fact that matters is that Nimmo does not abandon politics for religion but turns to religion as the sole channel for his activities that remains open only after he has, in effect, been rejected by politics. Again it is a matter of doing the right thing for the wrong reason. It is almost as if life in some dimly perceived way, is able to ensure that its ends are served. Men think that they are determining and pursuing their own ends but in fact are serving some larger purpose, for which role they have been created and for the facilitating of which they must suffer, getting what satisfaction they can from giving themselves up to their roles and not expecting any reward. Not every role is a beneficial one, Latter's being a case in point. He has the misfortune of being unable to mature and does more harm than good, but this only means that life is an untidy and wasteful affair, which is in any case self-evident, and no respecter of persons.

The Second Trilogy is a pessimistic piece of writing in that it reveals man caught up in a dilemma that he cannot resolve since the justification that the characters desire so much can never be achieved. They cannot hope to do more than convince a minority of their supposed readers, and the reception of the books by actual readers indicates that Cary has shared their lack of success. Few seem to have found much that is admirable in them, and it is easy to see why. Unsolicited attempts at self-justification usually arouse suspicion. No man can hope to be a hero in everybody's eyes, not for long at any rate, and nobody can be worthy of admiration in all his aspects. Besides, value judgements are always open to objection, opinion is notoriously unstable, and the facts upon which valid judgements should be based are extremely difficult, often impossible, to establish to universal satisfaction. The ephemerality of the bubble reputation is well-attested.

Once again, however, it is necessary to remember that we do not have Cary's message in full until we have read him to the end, and that in his final work he does pick up the implications of what he has written and provides a solution.

6 Salvation

The title of Cary's last book, *The Captive and the Free*, is sufficient in itself to indicate that he has finished his investigation of the various aspects of his problem and is once more looking at it in its entirety. His sense of its importance as a necessary culmination and completion of his work is probably indicated by his determination to finish it in spite of being in the last stages of sclerosis. He succeeded, just; for though complete in its essentials, the text as he left it was a draft that still required revision for the press, an office performed for him posthumously by his friend and literary executor, Winifred Davin.

It is interesting to note that, as was the case with the second and third groups, the book does not follow end-on from *Not Honour More*, its immediate predecessor, and that Cary again goes back to an earlier work to pick up and develop a point that he had made incidentally to his main concern at that time. In fact, as with the Second Trilogy, he once again takes his main point of departure from *To Be a Pilgrim*; not, this time, from Wilcher, but from his sister Lucy. Unlike Wilcher, Lucy was not interested in the approval of her peers, but in that of God. When her brother asks her why she does not give up her life with Brown, she replies that it is because it brings her the joy of the Lord. Yet she clearly suffered in it. She despised her fellow-converts and made her husband's life a misery. She kept her son out of their clutches. Moreover, the joy she experienced was by no means a continuous state, merely an occasional ecstasy, but it made her, though a captive who acknowledged Brown her Master, free in a way which her brother, for all his success in satisfying the permanent in his nature, never was. In creating Lucy, Cary had both confirmed the answer to the problem of freedom that he gave at the outset in *Aissa Saved* – that true freedom is only to be found in submission to the will of God – and re-stated that answer in terms that necessitated neither hallucination nor death, Lucy's death arising purely from her stubborn refusal to recognise that she was ill. All he had left to do was to re-state his answer in detail and at length, which he did through Preedy and Syson.

At the same time, Cary was able to resolve the dilemma that had baffled Nina, Nimmo and Latter, for it is clear that justification, if it is to exist, must be removed from the uncertain world of men and based upon standards that are not only immutable but infallible, that is, those provided by the concept of God. Nimmo, of course, though he does not convincingly achieve it, is seen groping towards this realisation, and must therefore be regarded as a secondary point of departure for *The Captive and the Free*. He is brought up to believe in God, realises as a result of his father's folly in forecasting the Second Coming that God does not intervene in human affairs, turns to politics as a means of alleviating man's condition, suffers disillusionment over the Lilmouth strike, turns back to God by becoming a lay preacher, then back to politics with Nina as his partner and finally back to God again when political power is finally denied him. His progress through life is very reminiscent of Nietzsche's vision of man, in *The Birth of Tragedy*, as fluctuating between Apollo and Dionysius, though instead of adopting his extremes of art and the brutal horror of reality, Cary adheres to the medieval dichotomy of God and the world. The movement, however, no matter which version is preferred, is something that one gives assent to, and Cary's use of it to breathe life into Nimmo makes the politician one of his most substantial characters.

But in Cary's world, as we have seen, God is logically impossible, for a God who is not responsible for everything in the universe, including evil, is no God at all. Nevertheless, the logically impossible must be supposed to exist if man is to achieve justification, and it is upon this paradox that Cary's vision of life ultimately depends. Logically, there is no God, but we can only find satisfaction and the freedom that we need so badly by not merely pretending that there is, but by believing it too. Cary has often been described as a religious novelist, but in fact he goes beyond religion to a state in which belief and disbelief are equally real and equally necessary because neither makes sense without the other. Cary's weakness was that he was never able to appreciate the implications of his thinking. He was precisely a case in point, a man who was able to believe and disbelieve at the same time, and so it never occurred to him that his concept of God was untenable and that his 'proof' of His existence was worthless.

Consequently, the artist and the thinker were always at odds and it is this, I think, that has left so many people, who have felt his power as a writer, so puzzled as to what it was that he is actually saying. He himself did not know.

Cary's concern with salvation, for that is what the achievement of satisfaction, justification and freedom add up to, seems to place him more squarely in the mainstream of twentieth-century literature than has perhaps been realised. Lionel Trilling, in his essay 'On the Teaching of Modern Literature', remarks: 'the questions asked by our literature are not about our culture but about ourselves. It asks us if we are content with ourselves, if we are saved or damned – more than anything else our literature is concerned with salvation.'[1] Cary fits this assertion admirably. He explores the whole question of salvation, making, it seems to me, a good deal of sense in the process. The will 'to do what you like' is real enough, and though whether or not our innate characters of being are fixed to the extent that Cary suggests is arguable, at least to the extent that many would want to place much more emphasis on environmental influences than he does, that we do have innate characters is undeniable. The need for education for life is real too, as is the need for justification, and it certainly seems to be the case that in purely human terms life can never be entirely satisfactory. The case for God needs no comment: when the facts run out we have to resort to faith of one kind or another if we still insist on trying to make sense of life. A difficulty does arise, however, in believing and disbelieving at one and the same time. As a thinker, Cary solved it by failing, or refusing at some subconscious level, to contemplate a Godless universe. As an artist, it worried him, since, in spite of the fact that he made his initial declaration of faith in 1932, with the publication of *Aissa Saved*, it was not until twenty-five years later that he was able to re-affirm it in a fully worked out statement that does not depend, as is the case with Aissa, upon an abnormal state of mind for credibility and deals openly with man's need of God in his attempt to make sense of the world. For in Cary's world, the ultimate dilemma is not that man is condemned to be free, but that he is condemned to be damned unless he can find salvation in the illusion that God exists. The appeals to their fellows that Nina, Nimmo and Latter make are, in the final analysis, pathetic in their failures. In spite of their conscious sincerity, they reveal rather than conceal their faults, condemn rather than justify themselves. They cannot escape from the constraints of their innate drives towards self-satisfaction which are, paradoxically, incapable of giving satisfaction to them as social beings, simply because, in satisfying themselves, they inevitably antagonise many of their fellows. Success in the one way means failure in the other. The problem of the first group protagonists will not go away. It is a Gordian knot that, like the original, has to be cut.

The Captive and the Free deals with the necessity for the invention of God in two ways. Syson is seen being brought to realise the need and to perform successfully the act. Preedy, who has passed through this stage before the story begins, is seen working out the consequences of his unsuccessful attempt.

The search for satisfaction, personal satisfaction, of course underlies everything. The invention of God is a means in Cary's world, not an end. This is underlined by what he has to say about evangelicalism:

> evangelical sects in their first inspiration and vigour invariably split. Their strength is in the faith, the only true faith, of the autonomous individual soul; their weakness is in the difficulty of persuading such souls to agree on any dogmatic statement of their faith   (*CF*, p. 58)

This is to say that every man who invents God invents his own personal version of him, as he must if Cary's vision of man is to hold good. Preedy's version is thus not only different from Syson's, but different from Cary's too, for Preedy believes in miracles. He does not claim for himself the power to perform them, but does claim it for God, and he sees Him as being activated by the faith of the sufferer. 'It is their faith that heals', he says to Tinney, and 'it is only God who can cure. I can only try to put the sufferer in accord with the Holy Spirit. Without faith there can be no cure' (*CF*, p. 65).

The falseness of Preedy's belief is indicated within the book by the note to Syson from the mother of the girl Ada, who dies in spite of Preedy's ministrations and his conviction of her complete faith. ' "I know now," she wrote [Syson is reporting her words], "that you were right and that God could not save my poor child" ' (*CF*,

p. 284). Why then does Cary depict Preedy in this way? The answer would seem to be that in Preedy we have a character who, because he has not, in Cary's terms, achieved a full vision of the truth, serves to illustrate the success of Syson, who, by the end of the book, has. Preedy is perfectly sincere but, on the question of miracles, quite misguided, and he therefore sometimes does harm, by preventing sufferers from seeking medical advice, when he means to do good. Whatever the explanation of the cures, and Cary does, as in his depiction of Elizabeth Aladai in *The African Witch*, seem to regard them as real, it is not what Preedy thinks. Because he does not share Cary's knowledge of the impossibility of miracles, his God, like Henry James's golden bowl, has a flaw. Hence his periods of self-doubt when the cures do not come, and the controversy that continually surrounds him. Hence his refusal to be advised or controlled. He cannot compromise with the idea of the God he has created because his whole life hangs upon the inviolability of his concept. Either God is perfect or he is nothing and Preedy therefore cannot admit what to him would be an impossibility. The very manner of his conversion indicates the all-or-nothing nature of his religious beliefs:

> He had gone to jeer at a hell-fire evangelist at Hyde Park Corner, and had ended kneeling at his feet, the only penitent   (*CF*, p. 57)

> It was not by my own will, it was not by my own power, that I went forward that day to give myself up to God . . . I found myself on my knees in the dirt, and felt within a voice that said, 'Come to me – and I will give you peace.' . . . and I knew it for the very voice of God   (*CF*, p. 58)

The highly emotional, quite irrational nature of the incident is reflected in the language: 'give myself up' suggests the surrender of a criminal; 'found myself' reflects involuntary action; 'felt within a voice', instead of the expected 'heard', intensifies the experience beyond the possibility of being mistaken, and reinforces the element of irrationality. The whole paragraph, with the images of thunder, lightning, fire and destruction that accompany his realisation of his own fallen state, has even a touch of hysteria about it. Clearly, Preedy dare not question his own faulty creation, and therefore remains in a state of perpetual conflict both with himself, his followers and the world at large.

It is for this reason that the ending of the book is inconclusive so far as he is concerned, and leaves him embattled in a basement with the press and the public thronging the street. The scene has symbolic force. No resolution of his position is possible because his position is fundamentally untenable and he cannot modify it. Hooper reports him as saying: 'Either God has power to abolish evil or he hasn't, and if he hasn't then he isn't God, in fact there isn't any God' (*CF*, p. 54). He is thus in exactly the same dilemma that Cary himself was in, but takes the line that Cary rejected and has to stay on it in order not to destroy his own salvation. His effort to create a God who will enable him to justify himself both to himself and to the world is no more than a partial success. He is, in fact, a re-working of Aissa whose career is not crowned by a martyr's death and a saint's ecstatic vision.

It is Syson who achieves the full Carian vision. He begins the book as an aggressively orthodox clergyman with no noticeable powers of insight. 'Simply tell 'em Preedy is a crook and doesn't do these cures' (*CF*, p. 52), he says to his vicar. He is also pathetically naïve: 'He considered that Hooper was only a jour-nalist and that he couldn't know as much about the matter of faith-healing as a man like himself in the profession' (*CF*, p. 52); and ignorant: 'Like most people he had no idea of the law. He did not imagine for a moment that it could be illegal to tell the truth' (*CF*, p. 104). Like Preedy, he is perfectly sincere, but unlike him, he has not suffered a violent conversion. His approach to God is therefore rational rather than emotional. This makes him the more likely to change the nature of his vision, as he is dependent on received dogma rather than traumatic revelation. He has not yet created his own God, but is merely accepting the orthodox version for the time being. The crisis comes when he finds that his faith will not take what Cary described in the preface to *Aissa Saved* as 'the big knock'. In the extract from the book which he writes in prison, and from which the narrator quotes, he says, referring to Preedy: 'Those posters of his, those preachings, had shown me that my faith was a muddle of wish-fulfilment and time-serving' (*CF*, p. 282). The whole 'extract', though much too long to reproduce, is very interesting in that in it Cary makes Syson use the same arguments and ask the same questions that he himself used and asked in the typescript 'My own religious history . . .'.[2] Syson, however, does not repeat Cary's feat of solving the problem of God by taking thought. His revelation, that is, his own act of creation of a God who will enable him to justify his own existence, comes as a result of the note from Ada's mother, already referred to on p. 131. It ends, 'my husband has left me, and once I wanted to die. But now I am glad to be alive to remember that happiness when I had my child and to thank God for all the love in the world', to which Syson's reaction is 'when I read the letter, I was suddenly moved to understand the thing that had stood before my eyes all my life . . . the miracle of God's love in the world' (*CF*, p. 284). He has achieved Cary's own insight: that the proof of God's existence does not depend upon his ability to work miracles. The mere existence of love (to which Cary would add beauty and goodness) is sufficient. The point is reinforced by contrasting Ada's mother and Syson with Aissa. She was not capable, because of her immaturity and ignorance, of making the imaginative leap from the love of people, her husband and son, to love as a force in human life. They, although they both lose their spouses and children as she does, are. Ada's mother transcends the 'Cary woman' syndrome and is no longer the mere captive of her nature. Syson too, though family and career have gone, by realising and accepting the true nature of God, has likewise achieved freedom. Accepting God's will makes him capable of doing what he likes, because his purposes will henceforth reflect those of God.

The implications of this for Syson's daily life are not given. All we know is that he writes the book from which these 'extracts' are taken. The 'book' itself, however, may be seen as the fruit of a successful act of self-justification, just as Cary's novels themselves may.

The possession of freedom does not of itself, however, solve all problems. The smile of delight that it brings to Syson's face is misinterpreted by the crowd as he leaves the court (at the very beginning of the book) and he is attacked as a cynical villain by a righteously indignant member of it. Hence Syson's need to explain himself, and hence the book he writes in prison. The parallel between Syson and Cary himself at this point will be clear. In Cary's case, too, books had followed realisation coming at the end of a period of abortive effort.

In *The Captive and the Free*, he finally succeeds in conveying in his fiction how salvation is within the grasp of us all. Few human beings indeed are saints like Aissa, or innocent children of nature like Mister Johnson; few if any possess the invincible self-sufficiency of Gulley Jimson. The kinds of salvation they achieve are not available for the more usual kinds of human beings represented by Nina, Nimmo and Latter. They are special varieties for special cases. But the salvation achieved by Syson is within the grasp of the ordinary person. It can be reached through error and suffering, as Ada's mother and Syson reach it, or through long and patient thought, as Cary himself reached it, but no unusual qualities are needed. Indeed, as in the case of Preedy, unusual qualities are apt to be a disqualification. He is over-emotional and too clear-sighted, apart from being a spellbinder faced with the necessity of using his powers.

Cary's ultimate message (he considered that all serious writers have one) can now be understood. Man is condemned to perpetual conflict not because he is free but because he is both an individual, the prisoner of his own nature and education, and a social being who needs to justify himself in the eyes of his peers. His dilemma is that whilst he cannot help pursuing, or at least wanting to pursue, his own ends, he is intelligent enough to perceive the evil that so often ensues and to realise that this is often socially counter-productive. He desires to avoid evil because what harms others harms him, but he cannot help causing it, and as a result is driven to invent God, who alone can provide justification and salvation.

> For the good that I would I do not: but the evil which I would not that I do.
> O wretched man that I am! who shall deliver me from the body of this death?
> I thank God. . . . So then with the mind I myself serve the law of God; but with the flesh the law of sin   (Romans 7:19, 24 and 25)

Paul's words are relevant to Cary's world. God, though seen to be impossible, is nevertheless essential. The impossibility must therefore be set aside and life must be founded upon faith and, ultimately, therefore, upon illusion. The idea of God cannot solve the world's problems, but it can solve those of the individual, as it solves those of Syson and as it solved those of Cary himself.

Cary's vision is, in many ways, an unattractive one. The same need to believe that man is both free and moral that Cary experienced is very strong in most men, and militates against the willing acceptance of ideas to the contrary. Professor Molly Mahood, as I have said, has observed that Cary's vision is in some ways an amoral one, and clearly sees this as diminishing its value. No doubt Professor Mahood, in common with the great majority, takes it for granted that man is a moral being. In spite of that, however, Cary's views are undeniably plausible as an explanation of the observed behaviour of man. Human life remains the 'true chaos' that he consciously perceived it to be, but seen through his eyes, the activity that arises as a result of this is at least seen to obey certain rules based upon evident aspects of human nature: the needs for satisfaction and justification. Cary's world is not absurd.

The fundamental objection to Cary's work is that, assuming that the vision it embodies is true, it destroys the illusions (those of freedom and morality) that man lives by. He saved himself by refusing to let the theorist (the experiencer of the saving illusion) recognise what the artist was saying. But by allowing the artist to say it he has destroyed the possibility of salvation for the reader who regards his insights as valid. Once God is known to be an illusion, he ceases to be effective. For this reason, it is possible that Cary will never command wide popularity. Christianity is a declining force in Great Britain, but one suspects that belief in God is not. If such belief is in fact necessary to most people, the artist Cary can hardly expect to be thanked for pointing out its nature.

That he has done it, however, becomes plain when his work is seen as a whole, as it must be if its full impact is to be received. I have already argued that Aissa is saved, and saved by illusion, and in the full context of Cary's work this argument gains force. The only essential difference between Aissa's salvation and Syson's is that Aissa's God is very obviously a figment of her imagination and is treated as such with a touch of sly humour in the shape of the Holy Goat upon which Abba is seated as the book ends. The humour, however, is deeply ironic, for it is not Aissa's simplicity in misinterpreting 'ghost' as 'goat' that is being laughed at, but man's, and not merely man's but Cary's own. The artist is laughing at the theorist, for Aissa's predicament is that of suffering mankind, brought to misery and destruction by the need to obey the demands of its own nature but saved by taking refuge in illusion: 'goat' for 'ghost' is a deadly thrust.

At Syson's moment of enlightenment, the theorist has apparently been allowed to put his thumb into the scale, but by now it is clear to the reader who has understood Cary, and taken the unsatisfactory nature of his conscious beliefs into account, that this incident cannot be taken at its face value. To begin with, Syson says 'But God saved me' (*CF*, p. 283), and the knowledge-able reader knows that in Cary's world this cannot happen. The word 'miracle'–Syson, it will be remembered, describes himself as having understood 'the miracle of God's love in the world' (*CF*, p. 284) – acts as a warning. His miracle is only as real as Aissa's goat. There are other indications, too, of the parallelism that is at work. Aissa dies 'helpless with laughter' (*AS*, p. 212) though in severe physical distress. Syson is moved to laughter when he is reminded that he is a prisoner and goes from the court 'smiling in the most cheerful manner' as a result, only to have his eye cut by a broken bottle thrown by 'some true believer' (*CF*, p. 13), just as Aissa, crying 'Oh de joy, oh de joy' (*AS*, p. 211), has her limbs broken by the zealous pagans. Similarly, Aissa's departure from the world into death is matched by Syson's departure from it into prison and out of the book. The underlying similarity between the two scenes cannot be coincidence. Syson is just as much a victim of illusion as Aissa, and his salvation is equally as dependent upon this fact as is hers. The ignorant African girl and the 'free' man who achieves his own epiphany are essentially one. Syson's belief may enable him to cope better with the world than Aissa's did (that must be the implication of leaving him at large and happy), and is there-fore of greater value than hers, but it is no more valid as an expression of truth, which remains unknowable.

In the final analysis, therefore, God in Cary's fictional world is once again seen to be a concept devised by the individual to enable himself the better to satisfy the demands of his nature. Syson, whose nature is that of a fighter, uses his concept of God as a weapon in his fight with Preedy and when it fails him forges an improved version to enable himself to carry on. Fighting is all in all to him, 'the man was entirely ruined, . . . his wife had left him, with her children, and was suing for divorce' (*CF*, p. 13), but he is cheerful because he knows that he will be able to fight more effectively than ever. Although not Cary's most memorable character, Syson is nevertheless the ultimate Cary man. He has accomplished the greatest achievement of all, the completely successful appeal to God, and can face his destiny with confidence and serenity – until his new illusion fails him in its turn and he joins Nimmo in man's inevitable yawing progress through life. But with any luck he will die before that happens. Preedy is meant to be pitied. His inadequate vision cannot bring salvation of the kind that Syson experiences, and his future will be a mere repetition of his past. With Syson, however, the case is different. In terms of his immediate situation at the moment of epiphany he says to himself: 'though I was made free, yet I was a prisoner' (*CF*, p. 284). In wider terms, however, this statement needs to be put the other way round: though physically a prisoner, he was nevertheless free. Free, because his vision of God has had the effect of liberating him from the tyranny of himself. His own will has become synonymous with what an orthodox Christian would describe as the will of God, and it is this that makes him free. In doing God's will he is at last doing what he likes.

When Syson realised the implications of his assertion that God could not work miracles, he saw himself as a machine, and therefore at the mercy of his own nature. He says: 'And I could not bear it. I thought if that is true then I don't want to be made a fool of. If I am a machine let me live the life of a machine. . . . I had become a puppet pulled about on strings' (*CF*, p. 283). This knowledge, to a creature, man, who has the gift of illusion and who can imagine the impossible and the non-existent, that is, who can conceive the idea of freedom, is naturally intolerable. If man is to believe himself free, God must exist, in Cary's world at any rate. Hence, Syson's achievement of the full Carian vision of God restores him at once to both freedom and moral stature. He is no longer a puppet, and henceforth can do whatever he likes. The fact that his freedom is illusory is irrelevant because, like Cary himself, he has no doubts as to its reality. Illusion has become reality, for him, and doing what he must will henceforth seem a course of action freely chosen.

I want now to take up certain other aspects of the question of freedom and captivity in relation to the book as a whole. In his introduction, Lord David Cecil sees the matter thus, describing the free as 'following the call of their hearts and souls without reference to other people's opinion' and the captives as people who, for good or bad reasons, 'feel themselves compelled to accept standards and religious views inherited or imposed on them by society'. Cary, as his prefatory essay tells us, saw Nina and her son Tom in this latter light in *Prisoner of Grace*, and Lord David Cecil sees all the characters in *The Captive and the Free* in this way with the exception of Alice, Preedy and Syson.

I do not think, however, that these criteria are relevant to Cary's world. If they were, then Gulley Jimson would be the freest of all his characters instead of the most bound, the slave of the horse's mouth who defies society because he has to. The question of whether or not he wants to does not even arise. A criterion for freedom must be sought elsewhere, especially as only a brief examination of the five main characters in this book (Alice, Joanna, Hooper, Preedy and Syson), is necessary to establish that like the generality of Cary's characters they are all prisoners of their natures. The two women are simply further examples of the Cary woman. Joanna allows herself to become pregnant, like Rose, like Amanda, like Tabitha, like Nina, and for the same reason: it is her nature. Hooper suggests an abortion

> But Joanna, to her own surprise, shook her head. She perceived that this was something she could not do. The course of events into which she had thrown herself was apparently stronger than any consideration of prudence, or even of kindness to her mother. . . . She belonged to a process, a movement of life, which seemed to be stronger than her will   (*CF*, p. 194)

Like Sara, all she wants is a nest. When Hooper proposes

> Joanna was ready to accept him as soon as he spoke; she would have accepted him even if she had not cared for him, simply because he provided a way out of her worst difficulties. Marriage to Hooper would at once produce a normal situation, not only for her, but for their child. It was an admirable solution to all her problems   (*CF*, p. 234)

That Alice Rodker is also like all the others is not fully established until almost the end of the book, when she finally returns to Preedy, and the narrator suddenly reveals that

> it was, in fact, more than half true that it was she who had seduced him, who had insisted on being taken, who had defied him not to take her, who had put him into such a position that he could not tell whether the act had been more his or hers   (*CF*, p. 312)

With this revelation, Alice falls neatly into place and one is reminded once more of Shaw's *Man and Superman* thesis. Preedy thinks that she is 'now completely his in body and soul' (*CF*, p. 311), but he is just as much caught by her as Tanner is by Ann Whitfield and as Hooper realises that he is by Joanna. This is why Alice is able to say, after Preedy has struck her: 'I'm all right. I can take it. I've got straight again and I can take anything' (*CF*, p. 313). She is finally both resigned to following and determined to follow the dictates of her nature. Her attempt to emulate Amanda and be free by ridding herself of Preedy, brought about by his responsibility for the death of her child, has failed, and when Cary, almost at once, writes this: 'She tossed her head at them, with the universal gesture of the person who defies the world, the glance of a free soul' (*CF*, p. 314), he surely settles once and for all the question of freedom in his world. Doing what you like can only mean obeying the dictates of nature, that is, doing what must be done regardless of the consequences, for none of Cary's major female characters ever does anything else, and it is this that he now describes as freedom. In Alice's case, moreover, it is all pre-figured in her conversation with Kate Rideout:

> 'You'd much better make it up with him – Preedy's your fate, dear.'
> 'I'd sooner kill myself.'
> 'Tell me, did you make love to him first?'
> 'That's like the woman in the court –'
> 'Well, you were precocious – and mad about him.'
> 'It's a lie – I wasn't precocious – he hurt me – and I wasn't mad about him – I thought he needed me – it's what he said' (*CF*, p. 148)

It is not surprising that Alice does not realise the truth, but there is no need for the reader to share her ignorance.

Preedy is another version of the spellbinder and leader. That he is self-motivated is evidenced by his belief that he is directed by God. When he meets Syson: 'His offer of friendship to the man was spontaneous; as he would have said to himself, "God has sent me to him" ' (*CF*, p. 108). 'As he would have said' – not as the narrator says, for Cary, who is behind both, knows that God cannot intervene in his creation, and that Preedy is using the idea of God to justify the exercise of his own will. Once again, though, this does not make Preedy a hypocrite. Our society expressly tries to condition its members against self-interest and Preedy, like all Cary's characters and most people who are motivated by self-satisfaction in real life, and I again emphasise that the satisfaction of the self is not to be confused with mere selfishness, is forced to provide himself with a selfless motive for wanting to act counter to that conditioning. And what better justification for doing as one pleases is there than the plea that one is an instrument of some higher power? To plead the control of an earthly power is not enough, as many war criminals and terrorists, for example, have discovered. The authority of God, however, is harder to gainsay, and for a man whose nature demands the complete absence of restraint, it is the strongest plea of all. In this respect, Preedy is the ultimate in Cary's leader/spellbinder figures. He constantly and successfully insists that his actions be untrammelled. He comes and goes as he pleases; takes services or not as he pleases; refuses to account for money received; dismisses the Mission committee when it threatens to act contrary to his wishes; is a law unto himself at all times. Even Nimmo did not go so far: he was constrained by the forms of political democracy.

The informed reader has no difficulty in forming this judgement. Indeed, no other is possible. The question that occupies the minds of so many of the characters in the book, 'Is Preedy inspired or not?', is a non-question for such a reader. The claim, though sincere, is merely Preedy's means of achieving self-satisfaction and justification.

The establishing of Syson's fixed nature occurs when his wife, having returned to her parents, is reflecting upon him:

> she had always known of a certain desperation in his nature. The same quality that had made him a good night pilot, that had projected him so suddenly and unexpectedly into the Church, that had made him so energetic and unconventional a curate, could also carry him to suicide. For him every problem of life was a challenge to be defied. He was essentially a fighting man   (*CF*, p. 240)

This is, it is true, a character's realisation and not a narrator's statement, but it fits Syson so exactly that there is no cause to doubt its authenticity. He fights Preedy all the way through the book even though, as Preedy realises when they first meet, their fundamental positions are not dissimilar: 'I am directed now to ask you why you are fighting the Pant's Road Mission, for I believe that your heart is with us, I believe you are a man who truly desires to know God who is truth and goodness and reconciliation' (*CF*, p. 109). But Syson cannot defy his own fighting nature, with the result that when he is finally arrested at the Mission we find the narrator saying: 'It seems quite certain that he was out for trouble . . .' (*CF*, p. 284). And that this is his nature is made explicit by the omniscient narrator who, a little earlier, has already characterised his conduct in this episode with the words: 'He acted purely on impulse, impelled by the same mysterious obstinacy which had kept him for three days at the Pant's Road gate and hardly allowed him to eat or sleep' (*CF*, p. 280). In fact, of course, there is nothing mysterious about his obstinacy at all: it arises purely and simply from the permanent in his nature. His freedom depends purely upon his ability to make the imaginative leap that I have already described, and is not something that man possesses willy-nilly, as Cary believed.

Though of a different kind from Preedy, Hooper is also a central piece of Carian characterisation, for he too represents embodied self-interest in credible human guise. He is neither artist, nor conservative, nor politician, nor holy man. He uses no idea to justify his activities. He is simply out for himself, and he is not scrupulous as to what means he employs. He admires Preedy at first because he recognises in him a kindred spirit, 'a man after his own heart. He had made a position for himself; he had become a power in the land, without help from anybody' (*CF*, p. 83), but he turns against him. He has no interest in him as a religious figure and is concerned only with being the power behind the throne. He uses Joanna mercilessly until he finds that he cannot, after all, discard her, and continues to use her for his own ends even after this, as is evidenced by the final episode when he gets her to take him to Alice. He struggles unashamedly for power over the *Argus* and at the end of the book he disregards truth, or rather the disinterested attempt to establish it, by deciding to turn the final events into a piece of popular journalism. In this scene he suddenly becomes reminiscent of Wilcher in that he realises that there is another way: 'Hooper was suddenly tired and disgusted. . . . For a moment he asked himself if he could take another line' (*CF*, p. 316), but the questions he asks himself are purely rhetorical. Like Wilcher, he cannot act out of character.

The question now remains to be answered: who are the free? In this book – only Syson and Ada's mother. In the whole of Cary's work – only these two and Aissa, and they only in the sense described. There is, however, another sense in which this question can be discussed, and it arises when a comparison is made between Cary's major characters and the implied mass of the population, those like Hooper's father:

> a steady worker, but completely devoid of ambition; a man whose only interests were football, darts, his pub-friends. A sober, decent fellow, not only without any general interests, but without curiosity. . . . [He] . . . looked upon [his son] as a weakling, a traitor to his class.
>
> That was why Hooper looked upon the workers with contempt and fear as the enemies of every good thing in life   (*CF*, p. 85)

These surely are Cary's 'captives', those who do not need to respond strongly to the demands of their natures, because what they want is, in the main, what they are already getting. It is not, as Lord David Cecil claims, that they 'feel themselves compelled to accept standards and religious views inherited or imposed on them by society'. Hooper's father is an active defender of his way of life, and so are Nosy's parents in *The Horse's Mouth*, for example. They actively resist change both on their own behalf and that of their children. They do not need to be active, energetic, unconventional, daring, ruthless in the search for satisfaction, and they are therefore of no interest to Cary except in so far as when they are pushed by circumstances to a course that is not within their compass, their lack of vitality causes them to break down and they become the Edward and John Wilchers and the Tom Nimmos, the total failures of his world.

Lord David Cecil's other critical observation, again in the introduction to *The Captive and the Free*, that: 'His main characters are generally odities and outcasts, inspired it may be by some divine fire, but freakish, cranky, often shady and at odds with the conventional world' is equally in need of comment. He has something of a point, but he overstates the case and the explanation he offers, 'his absorbed and delighted interest in the working of human nature and especially of its extreme and eccentric manifestations', is inadequate. Cary is not interested in eccentricity for its own sake, but in people whose daemons compel them to pursue a highly individualistic line and who may therefore be what is called eccentric as a result. The distinction is a subtle one, but it is important, because it makes a large difference to Cary's status as an artist. A man who is merely intrigued by the freakish is hardly a serious artist, but a man who is trying to define and communicate the vital factor in human nature that 'gets things done' (both Hooper and Kate Rideout describe Preedy in this way) must surely be seen as such. Professor Molly Mahood's observation, also made in the programme 'Joyce Cary and His Vision of Life', to the effect that Cary was 'interested in energy for its own sake', likewise falls short of the mark. The type of character that Cary portrays is bound to be energetic, but it is the motivation, the workings of the powerful will to live the life in them as it demands to be lived, that Cary is concerned with. His characters are no more motivelessly energetic than Iago is motivelessly malignant. They are, with the debatable exception of Gulley Jimson, unconscious of their motives, but that is a very different matter.

The important point about Cary's vision of life is that the essential and continual change that is so necessary a part of human life is not brought about by the deliberate actions of disinterested and high-minded men and women of genius who selflessly devote themselves to the cause of humanity. Platonist though he is in the matter of ideal forms, Cary was very clear-sighted in the matter of Guardians. They do not exist. Given that his characters are not truly free, then change, and therefore progress when the two coincide, comes about as a result of the activity resulting from the active men's and women's attempts to satisfy the demands of their own natures. That is to say, it is a by-product of their essentially self-satisfying activities, the phrase as always being used in a non-pejorative sense. This does not make progress entirely a matter of chance, since what is good for the active ones will often be good for the passive majority too, who, when they see it, will also want it and will help to further it. Apart from this, man has an inherent disposition to seek his own advantage. This latter point is of great importance, since it prevents Cary's world from depending entirely on randomness and leaves open the possibility of the existence of a purposeful and beneficent deity.

This vision, however, does amend the usual concept of man in a way that is unacceptable to many. Presumably it was even unacceptable to Cary himself, which would account for his failure to recognise his own message. It is, however, plausible, in that it accounts for human activity in a way that cannot be dismissed. And if it leaves man to a very large extent without the freedom to do what he likes and at the mercy of his own nature, it does not reduce him to a mere mechanism. Arguably, he still has liberty (Cary's absence of restraint) in some measure at least, and can still determine to some extent how he will achieve his purpose of self-satisfaction. And he is still evolving.

To complete the point that is being made about Cary's characters, his concentration on the active and their sometimes eccentric behaviour is justified by the fact that since everything they do is of potential importance for better or for worse, everything they do is therefore of interest. They are the salt of the earth and their activities, no matter what they are, matter vitally. This accounts for Cary's vehement opposition to censorship. The millennium cannot be planned for with any kind of certainty. The action that is condemned today may be seen in retrospect to have been the one that mattered. The active ones must therefore have room to work and their activities must always be a source of fascination. This point Cary makes fully in *The Captive and the Free* with regard to Preedy, and we weaken the impact by putting the question in the wrong terms: is Preedy a fraud or not? This is a non-question. Preedy is himself and not free to be either fraudulent or genuine. The question is: what will the consequences of his actions be? Upon his attempt to satisfy himself, and upon those of his like, hangs the fate of mankind.

It follows from this once again that Cary's people really are amoral. Characters whose every action must of necessity be directed to the satisfaction of their own needs cannot be moral in terms of any definition that rests upon transcendental standards or selfless consideration for others. This is not to say, of course, that Cary's characters never perform good actions ('good' being defined as 'beneficial to third parties'). They do, and Aladai listening patiently to his people's problems and trying to help them is an obvious example. However, in the same way that it is possible to be good without being virtuous, it is possible to perform good deeds without being moral: it is merely a matter of distinguishing between the motive for which an action is performed and the effect of the action. Aladai, to pursue this example, is ultimately more concerned with satisfying himself than the people who come to him, but of course the immediate benefits of his action are real, which is to say that goodness is real, even in an amoral world. Even in an immoral world, which Cary's is not, goodness would still exist. The point does not need arguing that even the basest actions can, and sometimes do, have beneficial side-effects; that the most selfless and most beneficially intended action can sometimes do more harm than good; that good and evil are, in fact, inextricably mixed.

What we are invited to observe in Cary's world therefore, is not how the good are not always rewarded and the evil not always punished. We are invited to observe that there are no good and evil people, but only good and evil consequences to the actions that amoral human beings perform in response to the inherent and irresistible demands of their own natures for satisfaction. The book in which this process may most readily be seen at work is *The Horse's Mouth*. Gulley understands how the world works (in Carian terms) in a way that no other of Cary's characters does, and it is this that accounts for his total absence of bitterness, and for the fact that he plays life like a game, doing his utmost to win but accepting his defeats without the slightest rancour. All the other players want to win too and have just as much right to do so, quite apart from the fact that – who knows? – it may be better for mankind in the long run that they do. Besides, nobody can win all the time. Only bigots consider they have that right, and only fools complain when they are beaten by better or more fortunate players. This is why Gulley can attempt to cheat and rob Hickson on the one hand, and acknowledge him as a true patron of art and mourn his death as the loss of a real friend on the other. This is why he constantly admonishes himself not to become angry, and why he accepts that governments cannot behave other than as they do. He simply behaves naturally and recognises the facts of life. All individuals and institutions have given natures which they cannot alter. The good and evil are incidental. The one is not a matter for congratulation nor the other for reprimand.

Gulley is, however, a very extreme, perhaps the most extreme possible case, in that he is merely a personification of the naked artistic temperament in action. Nimmo, whose 'reality' is so very convincing, is for this reason a far better example. He does not have Gulley's insight into the nature of things; he does believe in transcendental moral standards and he does believe himself to be a morally good man, in spite of shortcomings, who is inspired by

God, the sufferings of the poor, the example of his sister Georgina and the love of his wife. Yet he does not carry conviction as a good man, either to other characters within the fictional world of the trilogy or to many of Cary's readers. But postulate that Nimmo is neither a self-determining nor a moral being, but a man who does good and evil incidentally whilst in pursuit of his own purposes, and he makes sense at once.

It may be argued, of course, that Nimmo must be moral because he seeks to do good to the poorer members of the community, for example. The answer to this is simply that doing good to others is not his real object. He is seeking primarily to do good to himself, to 'create his own world' in Cary's terms, and the good that he seeks to do in politics is merely a means to that end. After all, employers do not exist to give employment, which beneficial though it is, is incidental to their purpose, and an employer who knows his business gives as little of it as he can in relation to his turnover. In the same way, Nimmo did not exist to benefit the populace, even though the benefits he helped to create, including, supposedly, the introduction of old-age pensions, are real enough. True it is that it was the existence of goodness in the world that was instrumental in causing Cary to believe in God. But it is not necessary to call up God to account for its existence. Self-interest is sufficient, and this alone makes sense of Cary's world. This alone accounts for his optimism. Barring terminal catastrophes and given a continuing supply of physical resources, material progress may well continue. Morality, on this view, is superfluous.

Cary saw clearly enough that the evil that man does arises from the conflict of wills, but he did not realise that if this is true the good must inevitably arise in the same way. One cannot deny supernatural intervention as he did, and then claim that goodness, love and beauty cannot be accounted for by the operation of the physical universe. But though Cary the thinker was inadequate and inconsistent, Cary the novelist was not. He saw all the implications and he wrote consistently about them. That is why there is no poetic justice in his works, and no finality except death. In these respects he is much less satisfying than writers of the type of, say, Jane Austen or Charles Dickens, both of whom believe in moral goodness and evil, and reward their enlightened heroes and heroines with a fitting degree of happiness. He is less satisfying, too, than, say, the Conrad of *Nostromo*, who, for all his pessimism and the convolutions of his treatment of time, nevertheless provides a coherent, and by implication repeating pattern of events that gives order to the knowable world.

Cary the artist, because he saw that life is a true chaos, portrayed it as such. Public morality in his world consists merely of the efforts of the satisfied majority to prevent the dissatisfied minority from upsetting their lives. The question of whether they have a right to suppress the minority does not arise, any more than does the question of the rights of the minority. The very concept of rights is void. Both sides are behaving naturally, as Gulley realised, and when one side grants what is called a right to the other it is either acting under duress or is agreeing to something that it believes, even if it does not admit it, to be in its own best interest. In this situation of endless conflict the individual plays out his part. He cannot, as Freud would have it, justify himself by his heroic response to life because he does not have this kind of freedom. He is, like Peer Gynt, neither a hero nor a villain, and when life is extinguished in him, if he goes anywhere, he goes back into the ladle. Neither punishment nor reward awaits him. Even the question of whether or not he has used his talents is superfluous, since he is the prisoner of his own nature. In any case, success and failure are not his to command. As Tolstoy pointed out with regard to Napoleon in *War and Peace*, circumstances make the man as well as abilities. If, as in the case of the first group protagonists, education is lacking, or, as in that of Edward Wilcher (*To Be a Pilgrim*), it is misdirected, or if vitality fails, then failure (in the world's eyes) will result. If public opinion is not ready, as it is not for Gulley's later works, then again failure will result.

It is no wonder that man, thrown as he is into this state of affairs, should seek to make sense of it, and do so, moreover, in a way flattering to himself. He is not responsible for his own nature, and his education in the formative years is beyond his control. He reacts against his helplessness by defiantly assuming that he has responsibility for his own actions. Because he has, or at least appears to have, the power to choose how best to satisfy his desires, he assumes that he is free, that his will has causal power and that he has the ability to choose. This illusion (it is essentially what Nietzsche, in *The Birth of Tragedy*, meant by 'art') saves him from the horror that is life. It saved Cary: his illusory beliefs in God, freedom and morality enabled him to write and to approach, through his art, what seemed to him to be the truth, unpalatable though it was. It enabled him to conceal from himself the awful nature of his own intuition. It saves his third group protagonists from hypocrisy, whatever their real motivation. Nimmo and the others are justified by this belief in themselves. In fact, Cary's work can stand as an exemplification of Nietzsche's dictum that art, not ethics, is man's essential metaphysical activity, if the definition of art is widened to include all forms of self-delusion, including God.

That the art of fiction is something that we habitually practise upon ourselves has been something of a commonplace in twentieth-century literature and is supported not merely by such humorous treatments of it as James Thurber's Walter Mitty, but by so eminent a critic as Professor Barbara Hardy. In her article 'Tellers and Listeners, Internal Narrative in *Mansfield Park* and *Persuasion*',[3] she says:

> We cannot take a step, in life or literature, without using an image. It is hard to take more than a step without narrating. . . . We cannot take many steps without narrating something of the past or the future. . . .
> The stories of our days and the stories in our days are joined in that autobiography we are all engaged in making and remaking, as long as we live, which we never complete, though we all know how it will end   (pp. 3–4)

She also says:

> In this narrative, it is often hard to make that distinction between truth and fantasy which we make more confidently in our judgements of literary story. . . . We may try to tell all, in true confession, or refuse to do more than tell the story of the weather, the car or the food   (p. 4)

Professor Hardy sees this phenomenon as an essential means of coping with life and of attempting to discern truth, which cannot be directly apprehended. It may equally well, however, be seen as a means of avoiding truth which would be too painful for acceptance. Ibsen long ago pointed out in *The Wild Duck* that the truth is often best left alone. Man has both the ability to conceive the non-existent and the impossible and the need to believe in them passionately, and it is sometimes only by so doing and by rejecting unacceptable though plausible ideas that life is made tolerable.

Given the need for satisfaction and the need for justification, and given that the active search for satisfaction must often necessitate action contrary to the wishes of other people and harmful to their welfare, then the life lived by illusion becomes not merely a possibility but a necessity. It is the equivalent of good manners in society. Communal life would be impossible without it. Morality and freedom then fall into place as necessary components of the illusion. Morality is the means by which we justify ourselves whenever we can, falling back upon the plea of necessity only when we must. The concept of freedom is a necessary adjunct to morality and one that can be used to justify us in restraining others from doing what is contrary to our own best interests: it is only if criminals are free not to commit crimes that we can claim moral justification for putting them into prison.

In Cary's fictional world, then, morality and freedom are illusions which the characters use to justify themselves. Thus, it is because Latter believes that Nina does not have to misbehave with Nimmo and that her conduct is therefore immoral that he is able to see himself as an executioner instead of a murderer. Being hanged is a price well worth paying for the satisfaction of self-justification. Is it so in reality? The question is variously answerable, of course, but because it and those other questions concerning 'the nature of things' that Cary sought to answer will not go away, attempts to grapple with them will always have an appeal. Cary's attempt is an irritating one in some ways, not because it is implausible – it is all too plausible, to my way of thinking – but because, not realising what he was really saying, he frequently obscures his own message. His explanations are misleading and the novels themselves puzzling as a result. Once he is seen in his true colours, however, as a determinist appalled by his vision and determined to escape from it, he makes a great deal of sense.

7   In Conclusion

I began by suggesting that Cary has been his own worst enemy, and I now find that I need to end on the same note. In common with other novelists of this century, he wanted his readers to respond to his books as to life. Just as life has ambiguities and complexities that cannot be neatly resolved merely by taking thought, so, he intended should his books. As he put it in a letter to his first publisher, 'what I want to portray and convey is not to be grasped, any more than any other kind of reality, by the brain alone, in contemplation, but only by a combination [of] thought and feeling'.[1] His mistake was in his assumption that a combination of thought and feeling was sufficient. For him personally it no doubt was. His own grasp on 'the nature of things' unquestionably satisfied him. But, of course, he was wrong. No matter how firmly we grasp life, or what means we employ, it changes and flows under our hand until sooner or later we find ourselves holding something very different, or, if we are particularly unfortunate, nothing at all. To produce books that demand the self-same response that, willy-nilly, we have to make to life is therefore a very risky undertaking to say the least.

Wayne Booth, in *The Rhetoric of Fiction*, says this: 'the novelist cannot be excused from providing the judgement upon his materials which alone can lift them from being what Faulkner has called the mere "record of man" and turn them into the "pillars" that can help him be fully man'.[2] He must, that is, both provide the criteria by which his creation may be judged and, in so doing, indicate what that judgement should be. The strange thing is that Cary would have agreed with this judgement. In a typescript in the Osborne Collection he himself says, in anticipation of Booth by some eight or nine years: 'The reader will assume an attitude according to what they think is your purpose. You must let this purpose be known, preferably through their feelings, through an experience. But it is better to state it in the boldest terms than to let it remain vague.'[3] He could hardly have been less equivocal

151

than that, yet in another typescript (also in the Osborne Collection), consisting of lecture notes and headed 'The Approach to the Novel', he states: 'An important element in the relation between reader and writer is the amount that the reader knows about the writer and his work. I mean outside the actual scope of the work as presented to the reader', and he goes on to claim that 'A work of art, by its own nature, excludes most of its own explanation.'[4]

The fact that these conflicting statements occur in typescripts that both appear to belong to the same period (1952/3) would seem to indicate that Cary harboured doubts about the ability of his chosen method to produce the effect he advocated. If he did, he was right to do so. His method, which involved keeping himself out of sight above all,[5] was not such as would serve the purpose. Yet he persisted, presumably because he could construct novels in no other way. Perhaps, in some subconscious area of his mind, he was aware that the explanation that the thinker had to offer did not fit what the novelist had to say.

It is this state of affairs that I have tried to remedy. Cary, it seems to me, in spite of his shortcomings, is more than just 'a good read'. I should certainly agree with the frequently expressed view that his work is uneven in quality (though whose is not?), but he has, it seems to me, something of value to offer. He sought to portray reality, not as it should be but as it is, and if he deprives us of moral worthiness, placing us squarely in a world in which transcendental values have been replaced by the checks and balances arising from the conflict of wills, he also lifts the burden of personal moral culpability whilst not depriving us of our essential humanity. If he denies us heaven, he also shows us that various kinds and degrees of satisfaction are attainable on earth, impermanent though they all may be. Above all, he insists that life is for happiness and that our business is to seek it. It is not difficult to think of several more highly regarded figures in twentieth-century literature who have had less of value to say.

I have already said that had he lived, it is hard to think that he could have added to his canon. Having reached Evelyn, in *A House of Children*, he wisely refrained from trying to show his solution to the problems of the first group of protagonists in action. Having reached Syson, in *The Captive and the Free*, it was finally time to stop. Solutions to the problems of life are always theoretical: attempts to translate them into practice are never satisfactory. It is sad that he died as he did but fortunate, I think, that he wrote nothing more.

I am very conscious that in seeking to re-interpret Cary's work I have belittled his reputation as a sage. I regret this very much, but I really do not think it was deserved and I am convinced that it has done nothing but harm to his reputation as a novelist. In setting the thinker aside, therefore, I have sought only to do the novelist a service.

Notes

When full details of sources are not given, they will be found in the bibliography.

CHAPTER 1: INTRODUCTION

1. From an undated typescript headed 'Unfinished Novels' in MS Cary 249 of the James Osborne Collection of Joyce Cary's papers in the Bodleian Library. It was given as a talk on the BBC Third Programme on 14 Oct. 1956.
2. This remark was apparently made to Andrew Wright and is quoted by him in *Joyce Cary : A Preface to his Novels*, p. 26.
3. My examination of Cary's thinking is set out in full in my PhD thesis 'Joyce Cary: an Examination of his Novels in the Light of his Ideas' (University of London Central Library, 1978).
4. From an undated typescript entitled 'The Split Mind of the West' in MS Cary 247 of the Osborne Collection.
5. *The Process of Real Freedom*, p. 15 of the typescript in MS Cary 206 of the Osborne Collection.
6. Ibid.
7. From the typescript of an interview conducted by Dennis Gray Stoll and Colin McInnes, in MS Cary 237 of the Osborne Collection. It was broadcast on the BBC Western Service on 12 June 1955.
8. From a set of lecture notes variously titled 'Approach to the Novel or Novel of Ideas', 'Meaning in Art' and 'Life in Art' in MS Cary 238 of the Osborne Collection. The lecture was delivered in Glasgow, January 1953.
9. *Saturday Review*, 31 Dec. 1955, pp. 5, 6, 31 and 32. In it Cary argues that 'Parents, mothers in their own family relations, act as responsible statesmen. What is more, they practise the same policies. They deceive, they evade; in a word, they manage a situation. What mother would tell a backward child that it is a fool? To do so might ruin the child's only faint chance of some measure of education. Who has not promised a child going to the dentist that it will not be hurt? Who has not made promises that cannot be kept, changed his mind to meet some new contingency? All relations between human beings in a free world require continuous adjustment. Every moral problem is unique and requires a special answer'.
10. From a typescript headed 'Politics and Morals' in MS Cary 240 of the Osborne Collection.
11. 'Joyce Cary and his Vision of Life', BBC Radio Three, 27 June 1977.
12. From a document headed 'For Walter Allen. the permanent in human nature the frame of being' (*sic*) in MS Cary 238 of the Osborne Collection. It

begins as a typescript and ends as a holograph, and appears to date from 1952.

13. From a typescript headed 'The Writer's World' in MS Cary 243 of the Osborne Collection.

14. In *Beyond Culture* (Penguin Books in association with Secker and Warburg, 1967) p. 23.

15. The letter is quoted in full in Malcolm Foster, *Joyce Cary: An Autobiography*, pp. 449–51.

16. 'The Novel Today', in *The Pelican Guide to English Literature*, vol. 7, *The Modern Age*, p. 486.

CHAPTER 2: THE SAVING OF AISSA

1. In an unpublished typescript beginning 'My own religious history . . .' in MS Cary 293 of the Osborne Collection, Cary says: 'In order to exist, a man must have human characteristics as well as vitality; if either is destroyed, both vanish.'

CHAPTER 3: IMMATURITY AND IGNORANCE

1. See n. 10, Chapter 1.
2. In *Vogue* (US), Dec. 1953, pp. 86–7.
3. Cf., for example, *AS*, p. 17.

CHAPTER 4: THE PERMANENT IN NATURE

1. *Sic*, but a small 'c' seems to be intended.
2. The *Adam* interview, p. 21.
3. From a typescript headed 'Horse's Mouth: Introduction for Braille version' in MS Cary 279 of the Osborne Collection.
4. *Sic*, but presumably the punctuation should indicate that the sentence is incomplete.
5. Wright first expressed this opinion in *Joyce Cary: A Preface to his Novels*, p. 91.
6. Ibid., p. 112.
7. R. W. Noble, *Joyce Cary*, p. 57.
8. In the broadcast talk 'Joyce Cary and his Vision of Life', BBC Radio Three, 27 June 1977.
9. An unpublished article, the typescript of which is in MS Cary 239 of the Osborne Collection.
10. In *Literature and Life*, pp. 32–45.
11. See, for example, 'What does Art Create?', in *Literature and Life*, pp. 40–1, in which he claims that novelty is essential to man.

CHAPTER 5: THE NEED FOR JUSTIFICATION

1. Wayne Booth, *The Rhetoric of Fiction* (University of Chicago Press, 1961) p. 433.
2. R. W. Noble, *Joyce Cary*, p. 89.
3. *Saturday Review*, 31 Dec. 1955, p. 31.

CHAPTER 6: SALVATION

1. In *Beyond Culture* (Penguin Books in association with Secker and Warburg, 1967) p. 23.
2. See n. 1, Chapter 2.
3. In *English in Education* (The National Association for the Teaching of English in conjunction with Oxford University Press) vol. 9, no. 2, Summer 1975, pp. 3–12.

CHAPTER 7: IN CONCLUSION

1. From a holograph script in the Osborne Collection, quoted by Charles Hoffman in his *Joyce Cary: The Comedy of Freedom*, p. 2.
2. Wayne Booth, *The Rhetoric of Fiction* (University of Chicago Press, 1961) p. 397.
3. In MS Cary 238. There is no heading.
4. In MS Cary 238.
5. In 'The Way a Novel Gets Written' (*Harper's Magazine*, vol. cc, Feb. 1950) pp. 87–93, he says: 'I try . . . above all to keep out of sight. An author has no more business in a book than the microphone on the screen.'

Select Bibliography

I have confined myself to what I have consulted, and in so doing I acknowledge my indebtedness to the authors concerned. There is a full bibliography of Cary's published work and a useful bibliography of background material in Barbara Fisher, *Joyce Cary: The Writer and his Theme*.

WORKS BY JOYCE CARY

1. *Novels (in order of initial publication, and indicating the edition cited)*

Aissa Saved (1932), Carfax edition (London: Michael Joseph, 1952).
An American Visitor (1933), Carfax edition (London: Michael Joseph, 1952).
The African Witch (1936), Carfax edition (London: Michael Joseph, 1951).
Castle Corner (1938), Carfax edition (London: Michael Joseph, 1952).
Mister Johnson (1939), Carfax edition (London: Michael Joseph, 1952).
Charley Is My Darling (1940), Carfax edition (London: Michael Joseph, 1951).
A House of Children (1941), Carfax edition (London: Michael Joseph, 1951).
Herself Surprised (1941), Carfax edition (London: Michael Joseph, 1951).
To Be a Pilgrim (1942), Carfax edition (London: Michael Joseph, 1951).
The Horse's Mouth (1944), Carfax edition (London: Michael Joseph, 1951).

The Moonlight (1946), Carfax edition (London: Michael Joseph, 1952).

A Fearful Joy (1949), Carfax edition (London: Michael Joseph, 1952).

Prisoner of Grace (1952), Carfax edition (London: Michael Joseph, 1954).

Except the Lord (1953) (London: Michael Joseph, 1953).

Not Honour More (1955), Carfax edition (London: Michael Joseph, 1966).

The Captive and the Free (1959), edited by W. Davin, Carfax edition (London: Michael Joseph, 1963).

Cock Jarvis (1974), edited by A. C. Bishop (London: Michael Joseph, 1974).

2. *Other books*

Art and Reality, the Clark Lectures for 1956 (Cambridge University Press, 1958).

Power in Men (London: Nicholson and Watson, for the Liberal Book Club, 1939).

Process of Real Freedom (London: Michael Joseph, 1944).

Selected Essays, edited by A. G. Bishop (London: Michael Joseph, 1976).

3. *Articles, essays and interviews*

'A Child's Religion', *Vogue* (US), vol. cxxii (Dec. 1953) pp. 86–7.

'A Great Author Faces up to Death', interview conducted by Graham Fisher, *Coronet*, vol. xli (Jan. 1957) pp. 41–4.

'A Novel Is a Novel Is a Novel', *New York Times Book Review*, 30 Apr. 1950, pp. 1, 34.

'A Novelist and his Public', *Listener*, 30 Sep. 1954, pp. 521–2.

'A Talk with Joyce Cary', conducted by Harvey Breit, *New York Times Book Review*, 18 Feb. 1951, p. 14.

'A Valedictory of a Great Writer', based on written answers to questions, *Life*, 25 Mar. 1957, pp. 105, 106 and 108.

'Barney Magonagel', *New Yorker*, 19 June 1954, pp. 27–31.

'Cromwell House', *New Yorker*, 3 Nov. 1956, pp. 45–67.

'Horror Comics', *Spectator*, 18 Feb. 1955, p. 177.

'If You Could Face Your Problems Today as This Man Faces His . . .', interview conducted by Merrick Winn, *Daily Express*, 27 Aug. 1956, p. 4.

'Important Authors of the Fall, Speaking for Themselves', *New York Herald Tribune Book Review*, 8 Oct. 1950, p. 10.

'Joyce Cary's Last Look at his Worlds', *Vogue* (US), vol. cxxx (15 Aug. 1957) pp. 96–7, 150–1 and 153.

'L'Art', *New York Times Book Review*, 12 Mar. 1950, p. 8.

'Le roman à thèse', translated by Christine Lalou, *Les nouvelles littéraires*, 11 Aug. 1955, pp. 1 and 2.

'L'influence britannique dans la révolution libérale', translated by M. Bouvier, *Comprendre*, 13–14 June 1955, pp. 45–51.

'Look Out for Labels', *This Week Magazine*, 4 Jan. 1953, p. 2.

'My First Novel', *Listener*, 16 Apr. 1953, pp. 637–8.

'Notes on the Way: Can Western Values Survive without Religion?', *Time and Tide*, 9 July 1955, pp. 901–2.

'Notes on the Way: Faith in Liberty', *Time and Tide*, 16 July 1955, pp. 933–4.

'Notes sur l'art et la liberté', translated by A. Proudhommeaux, *Preuves*, vol. xlii (Aug. 1954) pp. 28–32.

'On the Function of the Novelist', *New York Times Book Review*, 30 Oct. 1949, pp. 1 and 52.

'Policy for Aid', *Confluence*, vol. iv (1955) no. 3, pp. 292–301.

'Political and Personal Morality', *Saturday Review*, 31 Dec. 1955, pp. 5, 6, 31 and 32.

'Speaking of Books', *New York Times Book Review*, 6 June 1954, p. 2.

'Speaking of Books', *New York Times Book Review*, 26 June 1955, p. 2.

'The Art of Fiction VII: Joyce Cary', an interview conducted by John Burrows and Alex Hamilton, *Paris Review*, vol. ii (Winter 1954–5) no. 7, pp. 63–78.

'The Censorship Plot', *Spectator*, 11 Mar. 1955, pp. 275–6.

'The Front Line Feeling', *Listener*, 17 Jan. 1952, pp. 92–3.

'The Idea of Progress', *Cornhill Magazine*, vol. clxvii (Summer 1954) pp. 331–7.

'The Novelist at Work: a Conversation between Joyce Cary and Lord David Cecil', transcribed from a telediphone recording made on 7 July 1950, *Adam International Review*, vol. xviii (Nov.–Dec. 1950) pp. 15–25.

'The Period Novel', *Spectator*, 21 Nov. 1952, p. 684.

'The Revolution of the Women', *Vogue* (US), vol. CXVII (15 Mar. 1951) pp. 99, 100 and 149.

'The Tough World of Surtees', *Sunday Times*, 14 Apr. 1957, p. 8.

'The Ugliest Trend', *The Author*, vol. LXII (Summer 1952) pp. 84–5.

'The Way a Novel Gets Written', *Harper's Magazine*, vol. CC (Feb. 1950) pp. 87–93.

'Tolstoy's Theory of Art', *University of Edinburgh Journal*, vol. XII (Summer 1943) pp. 91–6.

Vad Kristus lärt mig (Stockholm: Bokförlaget Natur och Kultur, 1957) pp. 34–8. (Symposium published in book form.)

'What Does Art Create?', *Literature and Life*, vol. II, addresses to the English Association by Margaret Willey *et al.* (London: Harrap, 1951) pp. 32–45.

WORKS ABOUT JOYCE CARY

1. *Book-length studies*

Bloom, Robert, *The Indeterminate World: A Study of the Novels of Joyce Cary* (Philadelphia: University of Pennsylvania Press, 1962).

Echeruo, Michael J. C., *Joyce Cary and the Novel of Africa* (London: Longman, 1973).

Echeruo, Michael J. C., *Joyce Cary and the Dimensions of Order* (London: Macmillan, 1979).

Fisher, Barbara, *Joyce Cary: The Writer and his Theme* (Gerrards Cross: Colin Smythe, 1980).

Foster, Malcolm, *Joyce Cary: A Biography* (London: Michael Joseph, 1969).

Hoffman, Charles G., *Joyce Cary: The Comedy of Freedom* (Pittsburgh: University of Pittsburgh Press, 1964).

Larsen, Golden, *The Dark Descent: Social Change and Moral Responsibility in the Novels of Joyce Cary* (London: Michael Joseph, 1965).

Mahood, M. M., *Joyce Cary's Africa* (London: Methuen, 1964).

Mitchell, Giles, *The Art Theme in Joyce Cary's First Trilogy* (The Hague: Mouton, 1971).

Noble, R. W., *Joyce Cary*, Writers and Critics Series (Edinburgh: Oliver and Boyd, 1973).

Wolkenfield, Jack, *Joyce Cary: The Developing Style* (New York University Press, 1968).

Wright, Andrew, *Joyce Cary: A Preface to his Novels* (London: Chatto and Windus, 1958).

2. *Articles and essays*

Allen, Walter, 'Joyce Cary', *Writers and their Works*, no. 41 (London: Longmans Green, 1953).

Allen, Walter, 'Joyce Cary', in *Tradition and Dream* (London: J. M. Dent, 1964) pp. 242–8.

Calligan, Edward L., 'Intuition and Concept: Joyce Cary and the Critics', *Texas Studies in Language and Literature* (1963).

Hardy, Barbara, 'Form in Joyce Cary's Novels', *Essays in Criticism*, vol. IV (1954) pp. 180–90.

Hoffman, Charles G., 'The Genesis and Development of Joyce Cary's First Trilogy', *Proceedings of the Modern Language Association of America* (1963).

Holloway, John, 'Joyce Cary's Fiction: Modernity and Sustaining Power', *The Times Literary Supplement*, 7 Aug. 1959.

Levin, Bernard, 'A Pilgrim's Progress to Joyce Cary', *The Times*, 11 May 1977, p. 18.

Levin, Bernard, 'Don't Take My Word, Just Read It', *The Times*, 22 Sep. 1978, p. 14.

Lyons, Richard S., 'Narrative Method in Cary's *To Be a Pilgrim*', *Texas Studies in Language and Literature* (1964).

Phelps, Gilbert, Joyce Cary in 'The Novel Today', *The Modern Age*, vol. 7 of *The Pelican Guide to English Literature*, ed. Boris Ford (London: Penguin, reprt. 1966) pp. 485–7.

Smith, B. R., 'Moral Evaluation in *Mister Johnson*', *Critique: Studies in Modern Fiction* (1969).

Stewart, Douglas, 'Joyce Cary – Protestantism', *The Ark of God: Studies in Five Modern Novelists*, W. T. Whitley Lectures for 1960 (London: Cary Kingsgate Press, 1961).

3. *Broadcast talk*

David Lytton, Lord David Cecil, Dan Davin, Dennis Duerden, Dame Helen Gardner, Sir Robert Lusty, Professor Molly Mahood, 'Joyce Cary and his Vision of Life', BBC Radio Three, 27 June 1977.

Index